Praise for *Forever Mom*

This is by far the best resource I've encountered for equipping and encouraging Christian parents at every stage of the adoption journey—from considering adoption for the first time to parenting an adopted child into adulthood. With *Forever Mom*, Mary Ostyn dispenses practical help wrapped in personal story with unprecedented humility, honesty, and hope.

—SHAUN GROVES, AMBASSADOR
FOR COMPASSION INTERNATIONAL
AND RECORDING ARTIST

This is the book that we wish we had years ago. Having adopted twice and housed countless orphans in our home through complicated times in their lives, we can understand what Mary talks about when she speaks of the deep pain in the heart of an orphan and the struggles a parent faces while trying to wrap your arms around them. But we could never dream that anyone would be able to speak to such complicated issues with words so clear and straight to the heart as what Mary has written here.

—LEVI AND JESSIE BENKERT,
COFOUNDERS OF BRING LOVE IN,
A FAMILY CREATION PROJECT IN
ETHIOPIA, HTTP://BRINGLOVE.IN

Mary Ostyn is the mom you wish would mentor you in your adoption journey, and she does through this encouraging and practical book. *Forever Mom* is *packed* with information you will inhale and then reach for again.

—LISA QUALLS, BLOGGER AT
ONETHANKFULMOM.COM

Finally a book that I can recommend to adoptive moms in different seasons—from moms considering adoption to moms home with their children for many years! Mary's authenticity and vulnerability to the realities of daily life as an adoptive mom is a breath of fresh air reminding me that each of my children is so different—based in not only how God created them but also how their pasts have shaped them.

—ANDREA YOUNG, FOUNDER OF THE
CREATED FOR CARE RETREATS FOR
FOSTER AND ADOPTIVE MOTHERS

Forever Mom is full of deep encouragement from one mom to another. Mary shines light on the painful loss and gracious beauty that are intertwined together in adoption. . . . she reminds us *who* it is that walks with us and gives us hope.

—SHELLY ROBERTS, SPEAKER AND
AUTHOR OF *31 NUGGETS OF HOPE: FOR
MOMS WHO SAID YES TO THE FATHERLESS*

Mary Ostyn's *Forever Mom* shines with hope, and is the book I wish I'd had when I first began my own adoption journey. Her candor, warmth, realism, and practical wisdom will inspire and prepare the family just now considering adoption, and experienced adoptive families will know they've gained a friend in the trenches.

—BRIANNA HELDT, BLOGGER
AT BRIANNAHELDT.COM

Forever Mom has joined my list of must reads for adoptive parents. Readers will enjoy the straight-forward but charming way Mary shares her first-hand knowledge. Even veteran adoptive parents can gain new wisdom and encouragement from *Forever Mom*.

—JULIE GUMM, AUTHOR OF *YOU CAN
ADOPT WITHOUT DEBT: CREATIVE WAYS
TO COVER THE COST OF ADOPTION*

Finally! A cleansing breath of fresh air among a slew of how-to books on adoption. Mary so tenderly yet expertly offers real wisdom, tangible advice, and realistic and effective means to assist adoptive parents as we navigate the trenches of helping our adopted children heal and blossom. . . . *Forever Mom* should be placed in the hands of any person who feels the call to foster or adopt or those who simply walk alongside those who do.

—HEIDI WEIMER, AUTHOR AND
BLOGGER AT OUTOFSHEMIND.COM

Forever Mom is the real deal. . . . God's grace and redemptive love flood her story. Her commitment to connection with each of her children offers encouragement and practical strategies to the new mom, adoptee expectant mom, or to those of us who are more seasoned on this parenting journey. I'll be recommending this book to all of my parent training clients.

—DEBRA DELULIO JONES, M ED,
DIRECTOR OF PARENTING ADOPTEES
CAN TRUST (PACT) AND AUTHOR OF
*GOD, ARE YOU NICE OR MEAN: TRUSTING
GOD . . . AFTER THE ORPHANAGE*

Forever Mom will refresh your adoptive-mama soul. Mary is courageously honest about the struggles adoptive families may face. Fiercely committed to loving her children even when it meant changing her parenting paradigm, she is exceedingly empathetic and encouraging as she offers her compassionate words of wisdom for those of us who find ourselves in similar places. Truly an inspiring read for every "forever mom."

—JEN SUMMERS, BLOGGER
AT HISGRACEHISGLORY.
BLOGSPOT.COM

If you are thinking about adoption, I highly recommend this book—you will want to keep it on hand to read and reread for many years to come. If you have already adopted like me, you will find yourself greatly encouraged and re-inspired—and also wishing that Mary lived next door to you! *Forever Mom* is a wonderful God-given gift to the adoption community, a comprehensive and authentic must read.

—BETH TEMPLETON, BLOGGER
AT HOPEATHOME.ORG

I wish I would have read this book before we brought our children home and then read again during the first year. It's a great book to prepare you as you set out on your adoption journey, and even better to read in the thick of your parenting. Mary makes you feel as though someone out there understands what you are experiencing—the hard times and the wonderful times. I highly recommend this book for all parents.

—JAMIE IVEY, BLOGGER
AT JAMIEIVEY.COM

FOREVER
MOM

FOREVER
MOM

WHAT TO EXPECT WHEN
YOU'RE ADOPTING

MARY OSTYN

NELSON
BOOKS

An Imprint of Thomas Nelson

Published in Nashville, Tennessee, by Nelson Books, an imprint of Thomas Nelson. Nelson Books and Thomas Nelson are registered trademarks of HarperCollins Christian Publishing, Inc.

Author is represented by Miller Bowers Griffin Literary Management, LLC, 630 Ninth Avenue, Suite 1102, New York, New York 10036.

Interior designed by Mallory Perkins.

Thomas Nelson, Inc., titles may be purchased in bulk for educational, business, fundraising, or sales promotional use. For information, please e-mail SpecialMarkets@ThomasNelson.com.

Unless otherwise noted, Scripture quotations marked NIV are taken from the Holy Bible, New International Version®, NIV®. Copyright © 1973, 1978, 1984, 2011 by Biblica, Inc.™ Used by permission of Zondervan. All rights reserved worldwide. www.zondervan.com

Scripture quotations marked NKJV are taken from THE NEW KING JAMES VERSION. © 1982 by Thomas Nelson, Inc. Used by permission. All rights reserved.

Scripture quotations marked ESV are taken from THE ENGLISH STANDARD VERSION. © 2001 by Crossway Bibles, a division of Good News Publishers.

NEW AMERICAN STANDARD BIBLE ®, © The Lockman Foundation 1960, 1962, 1963, 1968, 1971, 1972, 1973, 1975, 1977, 1995. Used by permission.

Scripture quotations marked NLT are taken from *Holy Bible*, New Living Translation. © 1996. Used by permission of Tyndale House Publishers, Inc., Wheaton, Illinois 60189. All rights reserved.

Cataloging-in-Publication Data available through the Library of Congress

ISBN: 978-1-40020-6-230

Printed in the United States of America

14 15 16 17 18 RRD 6 5 4 3 2 1

To my children:
I began with the longing to fill your hearts
with the love of a momma.
You've enriched my life and grown my heart
more than I could ever imagine.
And along the way you've taught me more about real love,
the kind that can only come from Jesus.
Never forget how precious you are to me, to your dad,
and to the God who created you.

See what great love the Father has lavished on us,
that we should be called children of God!
1 John 3: 1

Contents

Introduction

His Kind of Love

THIS BOOK HAS BEEN ON MY HEART FOR YEARS, EVER since the very beginning of our adoption story. For so long I felt like I only knew part of the story. And—let's face it—the middle of a story often looks pretty darn messy. I kept wishing God would hurry up and get us to the "happily ever after" part so I could tell the story as I imagined it. Except God knew all along that it was a different story that needed telling.

At one point He used my dear friend Molly to point me in the right direction. She said that mommas like us don't necessarily want to hear the ponderings of a momma long past the years of active motherhood. We'd rather hear the honest thoughts and struggles and longings of a momma very much in the middle of it all. I realized she was right.

And since that sounded a lot like me right now, I began to write. And write. I hope and pray it blesses you. I've been praying for you as I've been writing! But as I've been writing, God has helped me see my own life more clearly, helped me better see my children's hearts, helped me become more the mother I wanted to be all along.

In the end, this book became not so much a "how I did it," but rather how I didn't have it together at the start and how I still have so much to learn, and yet look: God is here among us, alive and at work and powerful. He is making beauty amid the cracked pots and the broken shards and the pain of living in this fallen world.

I pray that as you read about our journey, you will be encouraged on your own path. But most of all I pray you will see the wonderful, amazing, redemptive love of Jesus. He has been so very good to us. And His kind of love is the only kind worth having.

CHAPTER 1

How Our Adoption Journey Began

It all began with an article in *Reader's Digest* about the lost girls of China. From there an Internet search landed me on a Yahoo group page created by families adopting from China. And there I sat for hours, reading postings from family after family on the journey to adopt the baby girls orphaned by China's one-child law.

Many of the adoptive families were higher-income professional couples in their forties and fifties, parenting for the first time. John and I, at only thirty, with four kids by birth already, didn't match the typical demographic. In 1997 Amanda and Erika were nine and seven, and Jared and Daniel were six and three. It was a busy household, and we'd been thinking for a while that we were done growing our family. But around the time Daniel turned three, I realized I didn't feel ready to be done with babies. That magazine article placed a world of motherless children before my eyes. My heart was seized by the perfect juxtaposition of their needs and my longing.

I thought of our spare bedroom, of the swing and the stroller in the closet and the bins of baby clothes on shelves in our garage. I thought of John's and my genuine enjoyment of our children, and of our decade of successful parenting. Nothing in life had ever seemed more natural to me. We were the perfect family to adopt a child.

John didn't see it that way at first. He was content with our four healthy kids and was baffled at my desire for more. For a while I think he wondered if I'd lost my senses. After all, with four children, we already had a larger-than-average family. What could I be thinking?

That was a hard time. Never in eleven years of marriage had agreement been this hard to find. There'd been times we'd argued, of course; we're both opinionated firstborns. But until now, when we disagreed, we'd always found a way to compromise. Except the kind of compromising we'd done before tended more toward where to move a bedroom wall or how to use a free weekend or how to spend $200. There was no compromise position this time. And though I was deeply longing for another child, I knew that to be fair to all of us, my husband needed to be fully onboard, ready and willing to parent. The chasm between his feelings and mine felt a million miles wide.

When all my logic and all my tears and all my persuasion failed to move him, I gave up and just prayed. Not only for the baby who by this time seemed alive in my heart but for unity between us. If it was really God who'd put adoption on my heart, He was going to have to tell John too. If that didn't happen, I was going to have to accept this was not God's will for our lives after all. Either occurrence would take a miracle.

So I waited. Prayed, fiercely at times. Over and over again I released my dream baby into the hands of God. I wanted that baby, but I wanted unity more. Finally, after an endlessly long, impatient wait, it seemed as if my miracle might be starting to happen. John began, now and then, to ask little questions about adoption. I'd answer, heart leaping hopefully. Then I'd mull over each casual question for days, afraid that I'd attached too much significance to it.

Then, glory be, he'd ask another question. And another. Discussions followed—cautious, carefully theoretical—leaving me simultaneously jubilant and uncertain. Could he seriously be considering it, or was my wishful heart running away with me again?

At one point we had a long talk with a family friend who'd adopted two preschoolers when her other children were nearly grown. We knew they'd struggled with one of the girls especially, but we were surprised to hear the depth of the mom's pain surrounding the experience. It was obvious as we listened that she longed for a relationship with her daughter but somehow felt thwarted, like there was a barrier she hadn't been able to cross.

Their daughter's relationship with her adoptive dad was easier and had much less conflict. But the mom seemed to honestly feel that she hadn't done a good job parenting this daughter. I couldn't imagine why she felt so conflicted, so torn about her place in her daughter's life. She's one of the warmest, gentlest people I've ever met. It seemed impossible to me that she was the failure she imagined herself to be.

I reassured her that her daughter loved her, thinking surely it must be true. I had had some tumultuous teen years where I didn't *like* my mom a whole lot, but I still loved her. My friend looked at me steadily, gently, not refuting me, but not agreeing either. It was as if she *wanted* to believe my kind words, but knew something about the relationship that I didn't understand at the time, and maybe that she didn't fully understand herself.

That conversation left me thinking hard, and I wondered what effect it might have on John's thoughts about adoption. But over the next weeks his questions kept coming. When he asked me what I wanted for Christmas, I boldly told him fingerprints for the criminal background check, the first step in the adoption process. Even then I half expected him to tell me again I was crazy. But somehow, mercifully, he didn't. My hope grew.

But there were worrisome moments too, moments all parents have, with kids fighting or vomiting or losing shoes when we should've been in the car ten minutes ago. Then he would turn to me in an overwhelmed huff. "We don't need another kid!"

"No," I would say. "But a child out there needs us."

I still don't know where I got that certainty. The fifteen-years-wiser me cringes to think of the pressure he must have felt at my audacious, impractical longing. Several times he asked me to expand my Christmas list, probably hoping to hear a more normal request like a Crock-Pot or a computer. I insisted that his fingerprints were all I wanted.

By Christmas Eve my stomach was all knots. I was praying hard for a miracle. But I vowed to graciously accept his decision, whatever it might be. Amid the happy bedlam of four excited kids ripping gifts open as fast as they could—oh, I was already *so* rich—John casually tossed a tiny gift into my lap. Fingers trembling, I ripped it open. Inside was a little gold key chain with a coin-shaped gold medallion on it that said, "God Keeps His Promises." I forced enthusiasm into my voice to thank John. Maybe I'd been hoping for too much. Maybe that dream child was meant for a different family.

But John was still watching me. "What's on the back of the key chain?"

Heart thudding, I flipped the medallion over to look at the back. There, etched in the smooth gold on the back of the medallion, was a single golden thumbprint.

My gaze flew to his eyes, and the radiance on his face told me all I needed to know. My miracle had happened. He was fully onboard, and was honestly, amazingly, incredibly just as excited about another baby as I was. Two short weeks later we were talking with a social worker and beginning our first home study.

During the home study process we learned that South Korea's adoption program might be a better fit for our family than China's. The cost was less, and travel time was shorter, which meant we wouldn't have to be away from our other kids as long. We submitted our application to the Korea program in February, and in July 1998 we were on a plane to Korea to pick up our son Joshua, both of us filled with a heady mix of joy and anxiety. Only later did we realize that our first, tentative adoption discussions that previous summer had probably happened right around the time that our son was conceived. God knew it all from the start.

It was a muggy day in Seoul when the Korean social worker came walking into Holt Children's Services' little reception area. She was followed by Joshua's foster mom, a soft, sweet-faced, grandmotherly lady who carried our little four-month-old son with competent affection. She handed him first to his daddy. John held out his arms to our little boy, snuggled him close, and turned to me with a radiant smile. I don't think he'd looked any happier at the altar on our wedding day twelve years earlier. We were a team, on the brink of an amazing adventure. Together.

The alertness in our little Joshua's eyes told us that he also knew big things were happening. As I leaned in to speak to him, he stared at me, big-eyed and still. But when he turned his attention back to my husband, he smiled. John kissed his head and handed him to me. Josh was tiny—only thirteen pounds at four months—but very strong. He could already support his own weight when I stood him up on my knees. The face that we'd looked at so often in pictures was suddenly alive before our eyes, and I'm pretty sure he was wondering about the pale, damp-eyed people who were holding him.

The next few surreal moments were spent getting acquainted and asking his foster mom question after question: what soothed him, how he liked to be held, how much he ate, and what made him smile. He'd be all ours in two short days, and I knew nothing about him. I wanted to know these details for his sake too. Someday he might want to know about his early days. These brief moments, poised between the old life and the new, were our only bridge.

His foster mom's voice was rich with affection as she spoke about him. She said he liked to be carried, that he cried if you laid him down, and that he woke often in the night. I reassured her that we were looking forward to every bit of it. After a checkup with the doctor and some instructions from the social worker, our first visit was over. Back home he went with his foster mom.

Two days later we returned to the agency. Soon he would be ours. Within minutes of arriving, his foster mom was dressing him in the clothes that we'd brought and wiping tears from her eyes. The way she spoke to him and the comfortable warmth with which she handled him told me good things about his first months of life. It was obvious he'd been well loved.

It felt like everything was on fast-forward at that point, probably to avoid prolonging the pain for his foster mom. Minutes later he was placed in our arms for keeps, and almost immediately we were escorted to the agency's minibus. As the bus pulled away, headed to the airport, Joshua's foster mom ran alongside the van for twenty feet, dignity forgotten, her hand on the window that separated us, crying as she ran. On the other side of the glass, I put my hand up too, heart aching as I cuddled the baby she'd spent months loving so well. Oh, how I had prayed for this child; he was my miracle baby. But the gift of him in our lives did not come without cost to others.

When the airplane left the tarmac in Seoul, I cried again, overwhelmed to be taking this child away from the land where he'd been born, from the mother who'd given him life, from the foster mom who loved him so, but not from the God who created him. Josh was sleeping, peacefully clueless, but my heart was ripped wide open.

Fifteen long hours later we landed in Idaho, where four older siblings and dozens of family and friends waited to greet us. Here was the flip side of our son's loss—this whole new family eager to embrace him in love.

And oh, we did. Our early days could not have gone better. By the time Joshua had been home three days, my heart knew no distinction between birth and adoption. I was head over heels in love. He was mine.

But there was no question about it: moving to America had rocked his little world. He had an exceedingly vigilant personality, and his foster mom was right about his sleep habits. It was six months before he slept more than two hours at a time. He needed lots of holding, lots of soothing, lots of intense mothering. But he was also exceedingly responsive. Within a couple weeks of coming home, he preferred me above anyone else. He needed me, wanted only me. That fact only bonded me more strongly to him. Oh, I adored having a baby again. He was the happily ever after I'd been dreaming about ever since I first thought of adoption.

> Kristen said, "I'm not sure what I thought it would feel like. I guess the closest way to describe it would be that I thought that I would feel like I was mothering someone else's child. I can honestly say that I don't view my son (adopted from Ethiopia at five and a half months old) as anything but my own and that I have no different feelings for him than I do for my two older homegrown children. I often catch myself thinking things like, *Oh, of course he's allergic to that—I am too.* And he does the same thing. He always tells me that he has brown eyes just like his mommy. I guess the feeling goes both ways."

It's this kind of joyous story that most of us adoptive moms imagine at the beginning of the adoption journey. We know there could be tough moments. But we're confident that after an initial stage of adjustment, love will win—that our new children will settle in and do well. In many cases, especially when adopting an infant, it really is that easy. But sometimes the story *isn't* as simple.

After all the struggle John and I had gone through deciding to adopt the first time around, I honestly didn't expect we'd adopt again. That was okay with me—I was so grateful for this chance to be a mommy again. For months after our little guy came home, I was so over-the-moon delighted with him, and so conscious of the miracle of his presence in our lives, that another baby was not in my thoughts.

But the longer our son was home, the more John and I wondered how life in our family might feel to Joshua as he grew older. Words from a *Sesame Street* song went round and round in my mind:

"One of these things is not like the others, one of these things just doesn't belong . . ."

Our son *did* belong in our family in every important way. But he was a visual kid, attentive to details, and by the age of twelve months, he was already tuning in to the fact that he looked different. Once, when we were out shopping after he had just turned one, he spotted a little Asian girl and said, "Joshie." He saw the similarity. We wondered if he would hate growing up the only Asian child in our blond, Caucasian family.

Fifteen months after Josh came home, I spotted a little boy on an Internet waiting-child photo listing whose photo did something to my heart. Also from Korea, he was just two months younger than our little guy, and was on the waiting-child list because he had been born missing one foot. At the time I suspected he had been placed on my heart just so that I could pray for him. But the thought came to my mind that maybe we were supposed to be more than prayer warriors in his life.

Remembering our many unhappy discussions the first time I broached adoption to John, I decided this time to simply stick a note in his lunch box telling him about this little boy and let him think about it. I was pretty sure he'd say prayer was all we could do, and I was honestly peaceful about that. But that evening when he came home from work, instead of being dismissive, he was questioning, curious to know more about this little one.

Our conversation ended with him asking me to request a video and more pictures of the little guy. Two days later the video came in the mail, and we sat down to watch it all together as a family. Halfway through the video John asked the older kids if he looked like a good brother and said he'd always liked the name Benjamin. I couldn't believe my ears.

Three breathless days later we were working on a home study, moving full speed ahead on adoption number two. Compared to the difficulty of coming to an agreement regarding our first adoption, this decision was breathtakingly simple. We began the adoption process in October 1999, and by January 2000, I was on a plane flying to get our Benjamin.

This time John stayed home with little Joshua and the other children, and I flew to Korea with my sister and my oldest daughter, Amanda. We knew that the little guy on the other side of this adoption homecoming was going to be much more aware of the change in his life. But we didn't realize just how challenging it was going to be.

We first met Benjamin at his foster mom's house, where he'd been living since he was seven months old. Before that he had been in a hospital. He was now twenty months old and weighed twenty-one pounds, all black hair and sparkling eyes, old enough to turbo around the room on his own and tell his foster mom thank you in Korean. We sat on the floor at a little table where we were served tea by his foster mom. Within a few minutes I'd coaxed him onto my lap by offering him cookies and toys out of my purse. Our visit was delightful but brief, and I wondered how he'd be when it was time to take him home. To him I was just a lady visiting his foster mom. He had no idea his world was about to change in an irrevocable way.

The very next day we met the foster parents at the agency to take custody of him. Benjamin's foster mother cried when she handed him to me, but he barely whimpered. Once again my heart broke for her, but oh, I was relieved that he seemed to be taking to me so easily. On the subway back to our hotel I carried him on my back in a Korean-style baby carrier. Though he was quiet, he didn't seem unhappy, even reaching up with me to hold a subway handle all by himself.

Everywhere we walked, people spoke to him kindly in Korean, leaving me wondering what they were saying. But when they spoke to me in English, there was always deep sadness in their eyes, even as they were telling me he was a lucky baby. Soon he would be leaving their beloved Korea.

When I set him down in the hotel room, he scampered around energetically, climbing up onto shelves again as quickly as we could get him down. I discovered that he loved French fries and that my heart melted at his twinkle-eyed smile. That first night, when I laid down next to him to get him to sleep, he wailed and wailed, but after a few minutes of crying, he curled up and went to sleep. By the time we left Korea, I figured we were on our way to good attachment.

The plane ride home went well, and once again we got a joyous airport welcome. This time the greeting also included little Joshua. Since there was only two months difference between them, they were almost twins. Both would turn two that spring. Oh, how they stared at each other at first, and within days were inseparable buddies. It felt incredibly right to now have two Asian faces at our dinner table; it seemed so good for both boys.

Once home, conscious of the huge transition that Ben was experiencing, I carried him frequently, rocked him at bedtime, and came to him at night when he woke crying. And cry in the night he did. But when I tried to rock and snuggle him, he howled and thrashed away. Then he'd settle down a foot or so away from my body and lay his head carefully on my outstretched forearm, refusing to get closer, but not wanting to sleep without some physical contact. I assumed it was just adjustment pangs and felt confident he'd soon warm up to me.

After a month, he was still standoffish and hard to please. He would whine to be picked up, but when I picked him up, he'd arch away and slither down my hip. Or he'd lean limply outward, making his body feel like lead. Sitting on my lap in the rocking chair, he would lean far away and have literally let himself tumble onto the floor if I didn't keep him from falling. When I pulled him close for a snuggle, he cried and thrashed as though my hugs were torture. He wasn't content in my arms, but he wasn't happy away from me either.

What was I doing wrong? I worked harder to connect, hugging him, rocking him, carrying him, instinctively mothering him attachment-parenting style (more on this in chapter four) just as I had all my others. But we didn't seem to be gaining ground. Just as worrisome as his rejection of me was the growing fear that my heart wasn't responding to him as it should be. Parenting him was exhausting. Instead of feeling all the usual in-love momma feelings, the ones I'd felt with all five of our other kids, I felt oddly detached, as if I was babysitting the child of a friend. I knew it wasn't just the difference between adoption and birthing a child. Falling in love with Josh had been effortless.

Guilt tore at my heart. What was I doing wrong? After reading more about toddlers and attachment, I paid closer attention to his behavior and began to see more clearly what was happening and why I also was struggling. When I tried to smile into his eyes—trying to make that heart-to-heart connection—his eyes skittered away, avoiding me. If I tickled him, he resisted laughter with every iota of his being.

He seemed constitutionally opposed to having fun with Mom, often sabotaging good moments with misbehavior. He'd pinch tiny bits of skin on my arm or pull one hair on my head—accidentally, I first thought. Except that those things happened too often to be accidental. It was all tiny, subtle stuff, barely worth mentioning, but cumulatively it left me feeling constantly irritated and rejected. No wonder my emotions toward him were conflicted.

When I recognized his behavior as a sign of attachment difficulties, I was both scared and relieved. Scared to admit something was wrong with the relationship between my child and me. But relieved that there was a reason for my feelings—maybe I wasn't really a rotten mom.

Attachment, after all, is a relationship—a two-way street. I hadn't realized before that a mother falls in love with her baby partly because of the lovable things the *baby* does in response to mom's overtures—nestling in, quieting when being cuddled, enjoying being fed, smiling and cooing, preferring mom above everyone. Sure, motherhood is exhausting, but the very responsiveness of the baby pays mom dividends and fuels mom's desire to nurture.

You don't realize how much the *baby* brings to the relationship until you experience a relationship where that reciprocity is missing. I was starting to get an inkling of the confusion our friend had felt while mothering her daughter.

So what was different between Josh and Ben? Babies do tremendous amounts of learning about relationships in their first months of life. They learn someone comes when they cry, that someone cares enough to help them settle when emotionally overwhelmed. They learn that they're not alone in the world.

Joshua had gotten sensitive nurturing from his foster mom during his first months of life and arrived in my arms primed for attachment. He already knew his part in the dance, which made it effortless for me to respond in kind. In contrast, Ben spent his first seven months in a hospital nursery, with caregivers coming and going, offering nurturing that at best was fragmented, and at times likely downright indifferent. In fact, he'd spent so much time lying in a crib during those early months that when he came home his head was flat on one side. He went to his foster mom at seven months of age and lived with her for a year. Then, just as he was probably feeling comfortable with her, in his mind she handed him to a stranger—me—and walked away. No wonder he was guarding his heart.

When I realized that his behavior toward me was related to a hurt heart, my heart felt broken too. But it also gave clarity of purpose to my interactions with him. Since he'd missed out on bonding time during his infancy, I became even more determined to give him time to be a baby. He was nearly two on homecoming, but for a solid year I treated him like an infant. I kept him close to me almost all his waking hours. I carried him in a carrier on my back while I cooked. I played with him on the floor. I fed him bites of food at mealtime and bottles at bedtime. I lay next to him while he was falling asleep and came to him when he woke crying each night.

I took his most challenging, pushing-away behavior as a sign that he actually needed more of me, and I deliberately moved in, pulling him up onto my lap and snuggling him close. Holding him close made him howl, but I persisted in rocking and snuggling him several times a day anyway.

Cuddling him seemed to release an incredible rage—he had mountains of fear and anger bottled up in his little body. But through his cries I'd continue to rock and sing and hold him gently. He'd eventually settle down and relax into me, even peeking into my eyes now and then. As the weeks went by, he began to be less resistant and more relaxed when I sat down to rock him. He began to let me help hold his bottle. He began to tolerate closeness, then accept it, and finally actually enjoy it. And as I rocked him, I fell in love too.

Sometimes I wasn't sure if I was doing it right. This thing I was doing was a gentle version of "holding time," recommended by some adoption experts at the time as a way of gradually acclimating attachment-resistant children to affection and closeness. Some therapists later took the therapy too far, restraining much-older children in non-gentle ways. Because of this, holding therapy isn't currently recommended by experts.

But my gentle version of holding seemed to be very beneficial for Ben. Sticking with him, cuddling and rocking him through a crying jag, seemed to prove to him that I was able to handle his negative emotions right along with his positive ones. Unfailingly his spirit seemed lighter afterward. His eyes sparkled. He welcomed cuddles. He was playful. He'd have at first hours and later days of better behavior. I began to get glimpses of the delightful child he really was.

After nine months, I could look back and see how far we'd come. We still had work to do. He'd sometimes relapse into avoidant behavior. It was very much two steps forward, one step back. But remembering how he'd been two or three or six months ago made it obvious he was so much better—smiling, giving hugs, even sharing laughs with me. It was harder and slower than I ever imagined. It took a full year of hard work after he came home to feel like we were out of the woods. But it was completely worth it.

Now, at nearly sixteen, he's a typical teen, a man of few words who still sometimes grimaces when I hug him. But there's a twinkle of affection in his eyes even then, and a rock-solid certainty that the connection between us is good. We are connected just as truly, just as deeply, as any of our other children. And that connection is all the more precious to me because it was hard-won. He is a joy and a blessing, and I'm so grateful he is my son.

I wish everyone's adoption story was as easy as ours with Josh.

But many mommas experience difficulties similar to mine with Ben. There are no guarantees on this adoption journey, even with babies adopted at birth. Is adoption worth it? Unquestionably. There's nothing I'd rather be doing with my life than mothering these kids. I don't know why God chose to allow us to parent these precious ones instead of their first families, but I trust His providence, and I see His leading all the way.

I have no doubt it was God who spoke to our hearts, who provided money and made paperwork flow in precise ways at precise times. In each of our adoptions, I can point to moments where doors could have closed but didn't. It is through the grace of God that we are privileged to be parenting our children. And it is also through grace that we will carry His work on to completion.

But as aware as I am of the gift that our kids are to us, I also wish I'd been better prepared for the complexity of the job, for the layers of emotion I'd need to sort through, both in my own heart and in the hearts of my children. Adoptive mothering is a much more complicated adventure than it seemed when I first began. The hard truth is that *every* child who doesn't get to grow up with his first mom has experienced traumatic loss. In most cases he's also had several other caregivers before we arrived. It's not our fault, nor is it something we were given the opportunity to prevent. But every wound along the way will impact his ability to accept love and enjoy a healthy, reciprocal relationship.

Facing Loss

When I first became an adoptive mom, I honestly wasn't ready to handle the whole idea of loss. In fact, it's why my husband and I requested an infant the first time around. We wanted to exist in our child's very first memories, and we figured that being adopted as an infant really was a lot like being born into a family.

Except it's not. Loss is there, whether we realize it at first or not.

Loss. It's a word that we who are second moms often don't want to face. If we've come to adoption through infertility, we're already intimate with loss. In some cases that might make us more willing to delve in to the losses our children are experiencing, to face them and help our kids assimilate them into their lives in a healthy way. But our own grief issues can also leave us less emotionally able to walk with our children through their losses. In our longing to parent, we don't really imagine ourselves as parenting wounded children. We just want to be parents.

> Amanda said, "I went into adoption still in full grief over infertility. I was a walking open wound. I do not know why I didn't go for counseling—it was possibly some level of fear over being thought crazy when it came time to have a home study. It was wrongheaded, in any event. It should be the bottom line for someone whose world was exploded when they weren't able to conceive a child. Get help. You cannot take adequate care of a needy little child if you are a needy adult."

Older-adopted children are likely to be grieving the second they walk through our doors. At times their overwhelming emotion spills over into interactions with us. Even a child who never talks about his past may have moments when his loss will be huge in the room. We may not be the mom who caused their pain, but if we're the mom in the room, we're likely to be the target of their unhappiness.

When children come to us as infants and toddlers, we often hope that their grief issues will be minimal. They don't even know what happened to them, after all. Their only remembered lives will be with us. Some infants and toddlers do settle in easily. But many children adopted as infants still struggle. And every child has moments when their questions have an edge of sadness. My momma heart aches as I reach for gentle (often painfully ineffective) words to ease the hurt.

It's a huge thing to face that the woman who bore you chose to step out of your life. And even when you're told that it was an adult decision made for adult reasons, it's hard to believe on a soul level that it had nothing to do with you as a person. Even in the case of a mother who died, the child may feel guilty and wonder if he or she could have somehow prevented it.

My first real inkling of the loss inextricably entwined with adoption came on that airplane flying away from Korea the very first time. My understanding got deeper as I felt the pain in our second son's heart as he cried and tried to push me away. Plenty of moms don't see the loss until they've lived with their kids in grief soup for months.

Adoptive moms need a bigger army of supporters than most, and I pray this book will be part of that army for you. I'm not writing as a momma who has everything figured out—mothering five teens at a time tends to keep a gal humble. Rather, I write to speak courage to us all, whether we're having a day where we clearly see our purpose, or we're wandering in the mothering thicket.

Whether we're facing rejection, treasuring eager little arms wrapped around our necks, or grieving with a child whose past still aches, Jesus is right there with us. He is the one who can give us strength to join with our kids and face their soul wounds together, strength to love them when we're being rejected, and then wisdom to point them toward Jesus along the way. Through Him we have hope for the future, even when the now doesn't look quite like we expected it to look, when the victories are longer in coming than we hoped.

But I am not here only to offer you caution. I also want to urge you forward; there's so much joy on this journey! The soul connection you're hoping for? It is completely possible. And the more prepared we are to love our children whatever their needs, the more effectively we can connect with them. There isn't a more important job in life than mothering. Although we long for our children to find comfort in our arms, for them to feel like we truly are their "forever" moms, most of all we want them to find their comfort in Jesus, the one who will never let them go. He's created them—and us—with priceless worth. He is the ultimate, forever Lover of all of our souls, and He will show us how to love our children well.

Father to the fatherless, defender of widows—
this is God, whose dwelling is holy.
God places the lonely in families.
PSALM 68:5–6 NLT

CHAPTER 2

Taking the Leap

AFTER THE CHALLENGE OF OUR SECOND ADOPTION, IT was three years before we seriously considered adopting again. By that time our youngest two boys were five. We'd survived them "helping" Dad paint the house, unrolling miles of toilet paper when nobody was looking, and dumping all the videos out of the cabinet over and over and over. Life was getting easier.

At that point we'd had four boys in a row, and our oldest two daughters, Amanda and Erika, were teenagers. We found ourselves longing to parent little girls again. And since our other kids had all been in pairs—two girls, two boys, then two more boys, we thought it might be nice to eventually adopt two little girls.

We knew we would not be allowed to adopt from Korea again due to our family size. We'd gotten a special waiver for Ben only because of his leg. Every country has unique requirements regarding family size, age of parents, income, etc. Since we were hoping to adopt an infant, we decided our best chance was an African

American infant adoption right here in the United States. We updated our home study and put together a photo album to go with our birth-mother letter.

The birth-mother letter was difficult for me. It felt like we were trying to coax a baby from someone: show your picture-perfect best to a woman in difficult circumstances so she'll let you parent her baby. But we struggled through that task and got all the other paperwork together as well. Our social worker said the typical wait for a match was three months. We pulled out the baby girl clothes and waited eagerly.

Four months later we were informed about a baby who'd had extensive drug exposure in utero. I was ready to take her, but John didn't feel peace with that scenario, and so we passed. More months went by. We began to wonder if we were on the right path.

After we'd been waiting for six months, I read on an adoption forum about a baby girl in Ethiopia who was born missing her right hand. Since we already had one child with a limb difference, she caught our attention. We called her agency and found out that there was a family already interested in her, but if they backed out, we would be considered.

Ethiopia hadn't really been on our radar before that, but as we waited, we did more research and realized that Ethiopia might be a good fit for our family. When we found out that the baby had indeed been taken by the first family, we decided to go ahead and get on the list to adopt a baby from Ethiopia.

After talking things through with our social worker, we decided to also stay on the domestic adoption wait list. We weren't sure if the domestic route was even going to work for us, but both the domestic and the international agencies were okay with us going ahead with two adoptions at the same time if it did work out. We decided to wait and see what would happen. Maybe we'd get our two little girls the very same year.

We completed our Ethiopia paperwork in late September 2003. One day in mid-October I found a thick envelope in our mailbox from our agency. I was puzzled; referrals generally come via a phone call, not in the mail. And even back then, when Ethiopian adoption was quick, this seemed too soon for a referral. I ripped open the package, and inside was a photo of a chubby, stern-faced toddler standing in a chipped metal crib. I first thought our agency had sent her info to us by mistake. We'd asked for an infant, not a toddler, and besides, we'd barely been waiting two weeks.

"No, she's yours!" chirped the worker happily when I called to ask if there'd been a mistake.

I called my husband at work and told him about this one-year-old little girl, fully expecting him to tell me we'd need to ask for a younger baby. Instead, he was overjoyed—couldn't wait to get home to see the pictures of our daughter, and then was all in a hurry to get things signed, sealed, and delivered.

My heart was still hesitant. The paperwork stated that little Zion was almost one, but to me she looked like a toddler, and an unhappy one at that. All I could think of was that terribly difficult year with Ben. Yes, he was doing well now. But oh, I was afraid to walk that path again.

I asked John about refusing this referral and waiting for a younger baby. He was shocked. "No way. She's ours."

I feared walking hard paths again, but his rock-solid certainty steadied my quaking heart. If he thought she was our girl, she must be our girl. We signed a sheaf of acceptance papers. I started to gather toddler-sized clothing to replace the tiny-baby sizes that had been stacked in the nursery for months. And dozens of times every day I stared at her picture, trying to fathom what was going on behind those huge, sad eyes. Who was this little one who would soon be ours?

Two weeks later we got an update from the agency about our girl. They'd decided she was probably six months older than their original guess, which very much aligned with my impression of her. With the four months or so of processing time, she would be about twenty months on arrival. *Exactly* the age our son Ben had been on homecoming. Again I pushed back fear and reminded myself that God knew what He was doing.

Meanwhile, our paperwork was still out there in the United States too. In November we got the call. A pregnant woman in Chicago had chosen us. She was due at Christmastime. If everything worked out, we could have a newborn around Christmas, then go to adopt our little girl from Ethiopia just a couple months later. A baby. And a toddler. Wow.

Every week the pregnant mom and I had hesitant conversations, two mothers in such different circumstances. She was a single mom with two kids already, intent on bettering her family by getting through college. She said she was sure she couldn't parent this baby, this little girl. My heart ached for her. I couldn't imagine facing such a difficult choice. But hope soared for us. A tiny baby.

Two days before Christmas we got the call. She was in labor and wanted me there. John stayed home with the little kids and sent our two older sons, Jared and Daniel (then nine and eleven), along with me to Chicago to keep me company. At the hospital, I installed the boys with Game Boys and snacks in a waiting room, a stiff rectangle of hard chairs with a TV on the wall high in a corner. Then I went in to check on the mom.

Deep in labor, she spoke to me just a bit between contractions. I felt a gulf between the two of us, a chasm that I didn't know how to bridge. I longed to reassure her, but my best words felt stiff and inadequate. A few minutes later the nurse asked me to go back out to the waiting room. My sons and I sat in that plastic corral of chairs and waited for a baby.

It was a strange, surreal day. A bit after we arrived, in came a man and two little boys and sat down to wait. We soon gathered from overhearing their conversation that these were the mom's other children, there with their uncle. The boys were clean and well mannered. I looked at them and wondered if the baby would have that one's nose or this one's smile. And how could she hand off one baby after apparently doing a capable job mothering these others?

When the baby was born, her family went back to see her. I waited to be called, trying to imagine what this mom was going through. And I waited. As minutes ticked away, uneasiness grew in me. When they finally called me back, the baby wasn't in the room, and the nurse avoided my eyes. The momma looked at me and shook her head. "I can't do it."

All I could do was nod. Of course she couldn't. I told her it was okay and that I understood—and oh, I completely did!—all while inhabiting a sad, slow-moving dream inside my own head. This year of waiting didn't seem to hold a baby for us after all.

When she asked if I wanted to see the baby, I said yes. The nurse led me back to the nursery and pointed me to a warming bed in the corner in which slept a perfect, sweet, five-pound baby girl. I touched her finger and tears fell. Of course this momma wanted to raise her own child. Nothing was more understandable. Even thinking about giving this child away must have given her many sleepless nights—I could only imagine the relief that soared in her heart when she decided to keep the child after all.

I walked back to the room and told the momma her baby was gorgeous and that I was praying blessings on her future and hugged her. Then I walked out of her life, blinking hard past tears.

The next day was Christmas Eve, and the first available flight back to Idaho was on Christmas morning. The boys and I were stuck in a hotel in Chicago until Christmas Day. It was the oddest Christmas Eve ever. We spent the morning playing video games, and the afternoon shopping at Target so we could each give one another a little gift, as was our Christmas Eve custom.

In the evening we attended a candlelight service at a church that just happened to be right next door to our hotel. God is gracious. We lit candles and sang familiar words welcoming a baby King, words that restored peace to my hurting heart. God is good, all the time. I'll praise Him even when pain comes walking in.

On Christmas morning we flew back to Idaho with an empty baby seat. I was never so glad to fall into my husband's arms. My husband and my mother-in-law looked at me, worried, wondering, rich sympathy in their eyes. I was sad, yes, but I felt my heart already turning toward Ethiopia, being drawn toward the little daughter waiting there for us. *God must think that she needs me, undivided.*

Three days after Christmas we got a call about another baby in another state. The mother had chosen us, relinquished her rights, and gone home. The baby was waiting in the hospital. We could literally get on a plane and go get her. My trampled heart leaped again. But John was adamantly done with the domestic adoption scene, and our social worker had five other families she could call about this newborn. I followed my husband's lead. For us it would be Ethiopia, all the way. I read my toddler adoption book again and laid suitcases on the floor of the bedroom, packing for our next adventure.

Who Are You Looking For?

In talking with other adoptive families, I've heard many similar stories of the journey toward family, with initial ideas being refined, plans changing, and doors opening and closing the further you get down the path. Sometimes the many options can feel overwhelming. Spend some time at the beginning of the adoption process thinking through your hopes and dreams and talking at length with your spouse about what might be a good fit for your family.

One of the first questions to ponder is the age of the child you hope to adopt. That decision narrows the list of agencies it is possible to work with, as well as the countries from which you can adopt. Many families begin with the idea of adopting an infant, and for whatever reason, more folks request girls than boys.

Making a decision about the type of child that will fit into your family can be very difficult. If you're open to a child past infancy, there are lots of options. In 2010, there were over 100,000 children in US foster care waiting to be adopted. Many (but not all) of those children are already legally free for adoption. Check out AdoptUSKids.org for more information on domestic adoptions.

Tracey B. said, "My husband was adopted from birth, and we wanted an infant. We decided to adopt domestically in the same town, so [our baby] could have a relationship with the birth mother, which my husband doesn't have. International [adoption] seemed to be a little too scary and expensive for us. Attachment issues scared me, and although there were no guarantees that a child wouldn't have problems, we felt that if we had a child from day one there would be less chance of it. Race didn't really matter,

but we did want a boy. . . . It just so happened that the birth
mother that chose us had a boy."

There are also older children waiting in orphanages around
the world. Many waiting children have special health needs or are
part of a sibling group. If you're open to older kids, siblings, or kids
with special needs, you'll likely have a much shorter wait than will
a family who is open only to an infant. But each age has its own
challenges. An older child might not wake at night or need diaper changing, but he will take longer to settle in and become well
attached. He may also have had life experiences that you'll need to
address and help guide him through.

Keep the birth order of your existing family in mind too. It's
not easy for a kid who's always been the oldest to suddenly have
an older sibling. Adopting a child similar in age to another child
in the family has its fair share of challenges too, both when the
kids are young and on up into the teen years. Double teen moods
and 'tudes can be just as challenging as chasing "twin" toddlers.
Many experienced social workers recommend not adopting out of
birth order, and there is much wisdom in that advice, especially
for families with young children. All children deserve a chance to
be the baby in the family.

Pray without ceasing, do lots of reading, and talk with your
spouse about what might work for your particular family. Coming
to agreement is hugely important here. Any new arrival adds stress
to your family, and you really need to begin this adventure in unity.

Jennifer said, "While we were still considering where and
how to proceed, my mom gave me some old school papers
[including] my autobiography from eighth grade that stated,

'I want to adopt from Korea.' The seed was planted many years ago when our vicar at the time adopted two boys from Korea. We also knew an older couple from our church who told us about their adoption from Korea. Amazingly enough, the day we had found out about my infertility diagnosis, my husband called me with the news of his amazing adoption benefit from work. God is so good."

Where?

Once you have a general idea of the type of child you're hoping to adopt, you can narrow down the country from which you will adopt. Look at the various rules and requirements of each country before you fall too deeply in love with any one country. South Korea prefers parents under age forty-three. China has a relatively high income requirement. Ethiopia has a family-size requirement that is sometimes waived for children with special needs.

Deciding whether you're comfortable with open adoption will also help narrow options down. If you're hoping to adopt an infant in the United States, you'll need to write a birth-mother letter, be chosen by an expectant mom, and (often) have some kind of ongoing contact with the birth family. Some first moms want closed adoptions. Others want yearly updates. Still others hope for fully open adoptions with visitation. Figuring out how you feel about these various options may very well steer your decision making one way or another. Whatever your personal feelings are about openness in adoption, keep in mind that research suggests that some level of contact with their first families can be healthy for adopted kids.

Many families interested in adopting kids from foster care choose the "foster-to-adopt" route, hoping that a child who is placed in their home for foster care will eventually be released and be legally adoptable by them. If you take this route, you'll need to understand that non-released children can be returned to their first families, or to members of extended family. If you can live with that uncertainty, foster parenting may be a beautiful way for your family to look after orphans. In general, kids free for adoption from foster care tend to be school age and/or part of a sibling group. Though rarely easy, this type of adoption is usually incredibly affordable.

Barb said, "My husband is adopted and felt that his adoption was a real blessing to his life. He felt the need to pass that blessing on. We began foster parenting when our birth sons were all older teenagers. I happened to be at the courthouse one day with a sibling set being returned to relatives. Our caseworker asked me to wait since another sibling set was coming in that needed a home. I took two little girls home with me, and after a tumultuous year filled with many ups and downs, they became our daughters! We've faced many challenges and expect to face many more; the girls have certainly livened up our lives after three sons.

"We were not planning on adopting any more kids. But God had another plan! We were asked to babysit a four-week-old infant by a woman from our town. Well, he stayed for eight days and then kept coming back. After seeing many issues with him, at three months old, the mom agreed to us having temporary guardianship for a month to help her get back on her feet. Well, he never went back, and fourteen months later, we did a private adoption. We love our kids dearly and are so thankful for the privilege of having them in our home. Is it easy? No, not at all; yet God gives strength, wisdom, and grace for every day."

What About the Money?

When I chat with folks about our family's adoption story, the comment I most often hear is, "We'd love to adopt, but we don't have the money."

I am here to testify that you don't need to be rich to adopt. Our first adoption in 1998 happened when our income was just under $40,000 a year. Our income has gradually increased, but we've never been far above the "125 percent of poverty" guidelines—an adjustable scale based on household size that the government applies before approving families to adopt internationally.

Though our income is moderate, God has met our every need. I passionately believe that it is God who put the longing to adopt into our hearts. And if God calls you to do anything, He will also provide the finances to do it. I've seen it happen over and over again, with others and in our own family. Over the course of our five adoptions of six children, money showed up in various ways. Twice we refinanced our home. Once we got an inheritance. With our final adoption, a book advance came at exactly the right time.

I've heard dozens of variations on that story from other adoptive families who decided they wanted another child and then left the finances up to God. He truly is the God who owns the cattle on a thousand hills. He delights in bringing children into families, and He will provide for all our needs after adoption as well. Don't be afraid to step out in faith when He calls.

Seven Ways to Begin Your Adoption Fund

- Clean out your house. Sell what you can on Craigslist. Then hold a yard sale, and ask friends to donate items to benefit your adoption.
- If you have a car with monthly payments, sell it and spend $3,000 on a serviceable, older vehicle that you own free and clear.
- Ask your employer if your company has an adoption benefit as part of the employment package. Many larger companies provide a benefit in the range of $1,000–$3,000 when you adopt a child.
- Investigate the Adoption Tax Credit. This won't kick in until after your child is home, but will refund your taxes every year until you hit the total allowed refund. In 2013, that amount stood at $12,970 for families with an adjusted gross income of less than $194,580 per year.[1]
- Consider working an extra job for a year or so before your child comes home. Pizza delivery isn't glamorous, but the hours are flexible.
- Many folks refinance their homes to afford the adoption with the idea that they'll pay down the loan once their adoption tax credit comes. We did this twice, believing it was a small price to pay for the ransom of an eternal soul. These days we'd probably stick with debt-free options. For more ideas, check out the book *You Can Adopt Without Debt* by Julie Gumm.
- Start an adoption savings account that will

automatically deposit a portion of your paycheck into your adoption fund. Add any unexpected windfalls to the account as well. Don't be surprised if more windfalls show up than usual. God delights in willing hearts, and He wants to see orphans in families.

Finding an Ethical Agency

Once you have more of an idea of the type of adoption you wish to pursue, it's time to look for an agency that does that type of adoption. Some agencies only do newborn domestic adoptions. Others do international adoptions, but only from specific countries. Often when adopting internationally, you'll need to work with one agency for your home study and another for the international component of the adoption. If you're interested in adopting from foster care, you'll need to have a home study done by a Department of Children and Family Services social worker.

Once you've identified possible agencies, visit the Child Welfare Information Gateway (https://www.childwelfare.gov/) and read agency reviews. Join adoption forums online and talk with families who've recently completed the type of adoption you're most interested in. Find out what average time lines are for this type of adoption, and ask folks to share their experiences with various agencies. It can be useful to speak with families in the middle of the adoption process, but it's even more important to speak with families who've already brought kids home, and ask for their honest feelings about the agency now that their child is home.

Online Adoptive-Parent Forums

- Adoption.com: http://forums.adoption.com/
- Rainbowkids.com: http://rainbowkids.com/
- Adoption.org: http://www.adoption.org/

Steer clear of agencies that promise you a child more quickly than other agencies doing the same type of adoption. Also steer clear of agencies willing to let you adopt two unrelated babies at the same time. Especially in the case of international infant adoption, fast placement almost guarantees that unethical practices are happening somewhere along the way. Agencies may be offering first families money to relinquish their children. Sometimes it's the agency's in-country connections that are crooked, with the agency being unaware, or at least turning a blind eye so as not to stop the supply of babies that are the core of its business. There are many stories of adoption being described to the first family as a temporary thing, with families believing that their children will be returned to them later.

Offering first mothers money or benefits to relinquish their babies is outright illegal in the United States and is always a bad practice wherever it happens. It increases the risk that the first mother will make a choice based on finances, not from the heart. It also increases the chance that shady facilitators will prey on vulnerable women for profit. This is a huge issue; money has corrupted adoption at some point in nearly every country in the world.

International adoption from Guatemala and Cambodia was

completely halted due to this very issue. When widespread corruption was discovered in Ethiopia in 2011, the adoption process in Ethiopia was also dramatically slowed in hopes of allowing the government to better safeguard kids from trafficking. You can go to https://www.adoptioncouncil.org/intercountry-adoption/country -updates.html for a current listing of which countries are open and which are closed.

When you're longing for a baby, it can be oh-so-tempting to choose the agency that promises the quickest results. It can be downright terrifying to hear rumors of corruption after you have money invested and possibly even a child identified whom you long to bring home. But we in the adoption community have a huge responsibility to hold agencies to the highest standards and to support only ethical adoptions.

It is imperative to choose an agency with a long, successful track record in that country and talk to a good number of families who've used them. It's not good enough to call the folks that the agency gives you as references—ask other folks via message boards and online support groups. Did the agency remain communicative and honest with families even after money was handed over? Inquire with the Better Business Bureau in the state in which the agency is licensed. Are there complaints? Pending lawsuits?

Be aware that smaller agencies often operate under the umbrella of a larger agency. Find out the name of every single agency and orphanage that will play a part in the process and make sure that all the agencies taking any part in your adoption have a squeaky-clean record. Keep in mind that every agency will have a few unhappy folks. Adoption is a stressful, emotionally charged experience. There are many paperwork hoops to jump through, and some circumstances will be out of the agency's control. But if it is a reputable agency, the majority of clients with whom you speak should be able to tell you good things.

Marissa said, "We planned on adopting a baby from the US. Instead, we adopted three older children (ages five, eight, and twelve when they came home) from Ethiopia. Scariest 'plan B' of my life, but three of the greatest gifts I've ever been entrusted with. Plan B came about as we learned more about HIV/AIDS and how these orphaned children suffering from the illness had just been granted waivers to be adopted into families in the US. We educated ourselves on everything we could (from their illness to the realities of older-child adoption), took a deep breath, fell to our knees in prayer, and jumped in with more fear than sense."

Special Needs

Part of the home-study process is the dreaded special-needs checklist. Pages of questions walk through many types of special needs you might be willing to consider. Club feet? Cleft palate? Prematurity? Drug exposure in utero? What about a sibling group? These are surprisingly hard questions to answer, especially when you realize you are saying no to real, live children with each *no* that you check off.

Some issues might not even be on that checklist. For example, a child who has had six caregivers in three years of life may have some serious attachment issues that will take years to work through. So might a newborn, for that matter. On the other hand, an HIV-positive child with a resilient temperament might only need daily meds and a few extra medical appointments each year.

Right now there is a movement to adopt kids with Down syndrome who are waiting in orphanages around the world. Many families are truly passionate about such ministries. Pray and learn and see where God leads. I love seeing how God ignites different passions in different hearts.

Kristi said, "We adopted from Ethiopia four years ago. We had two bio kids and had never even thought of adopting until we both heard numerous programs on the Christian radio station during National Adoption Month. We didn't know the other was listening, and when I approached my husband about the topic, he just grinned and told me he had heard it too! We went to an agency that had an informative seminar on all types of adoption. We left there sure that [due to various factors] Ethiopia was the right fit for us. In the end, though, after having our son home for four years we know that it was God who chose him for our family. We were never in control! We are starting our second adoption. . . . Our new daughter has Down syndrome and is from Ukraine. God opened our hearts for children that are disregarded by others. It is not poverty that leaves our daughter orphaned. It is that no one WANTS her. Well, now we WANT her. We are so thrilled to be on this journey again!"

Often parents' feelings about their own abilities grow and change as they learn more about various issues. With our first adoption, we were open to almost zero special needs. We felt guilt pangs as we checked *no* over and over on the pesky special needs form, but at that point we were just brave enough to adopt, and weren't quite ready to face the idea of a child with challenges.

Once we got Josh home from Korea, God kept bringing people into our lives who'd adopted kids with missing limbs and found that kids with prosthetics learn to get around and live completely normal lives. By the time we learned about Ben, we felt comfortable with his leg. That first year home with him *was* difficult—but that was due to attachment issues.

Thanks to good insurance and a great prosthetics professional, Ben's needs ended up being very doable for our family.[2] Now, as a teen, Ben understandably has days when he thinks his prosthetic is a pain. But he does everything any teen can do, and except for a few visits a year to get his prosthetic tweaked, parenting him is just like parenting any kid.

Nancy, who blogs at www.indiatoappleton.blogspot.com, said, "Our church supports two native-born missionaries in India, and one Sunday they were visiting our church. They talked about a new baby home they'd started to take in infant girls who had been abandoned at birth and left to die. My heart began beating wildly. I spoke with them after the service about whether they were seeking families to adopt the girls. My husband and I weren't sitting together because he was part of the worship team that day . . . but after the service, he told me that he had talked to them too, asking whether they were looking for families for the girls! We both felt that God was clearly telling us that our next child or children were waiting in India. Our first daughter joined us in December of 2007, and we hope to bring home our two-year-old later this year. I will never forget the day when my sweet husband grabbed my hands in our church lobby, and we both blurted out, 'I know I should've waited to talk to you first, but . . .' That moment started a journey that we're still on, and I wouldn't change it for the world."

The Home Study

Once you've decided on international versus domestic adoption, considered infant versus older child, sorted out the money, and hashed out your feelings regarding special needs, it's time to prepare for the home study. When folks hear the words *home study*, they often imagine an uber-picky person who stalks around the house with white gloves looking for dust on the mantel and mold in the shower.

Before our first home study, I bleached the grout in our shower with a toothbrush. (Not kidding!) The social worker never even walked into that room. By the time our fifth home study rolled around, I'd figured out that social workers are friends, not foes, and was much more laid-back. However, one time, a couple hours before the social worker came, I went into the baby's room to open a rarely raised shade. That's when I discovered the back of the shade had been pressed against the window, had gotten condensation on it, and now was moldy. I spent a frenzied fifteen minutes (yes, again!) with bleach and a toothbrush before I finally tossed the shade in the trash and sent my husband to buy a new one.

In reality, social workers are *not* there to white-glove your house. They just need to make sure the home is reasonably safe for a child, talk with you about issues surrounding adoption, and then write up a report to inform the placing agency. Your social worker will likely talk about issues of race, discuss attachment, and recommend books to read. Read them! Read as much as you can about adoption and attachment so you can begin to think through some of the stresses that a newly arrived child might have. The more you know, the better prepared you'll be for any issues your child might have. (See appendix A for my favorite adoption reads.)

Getting Support Systems in Place

Before your child comes home, it's wise to assemble some support for the transition period. Most experts advise families to have a quiet first few months to cocoon, where you stay close to home with your new child and really focus on getting to know one another. It's wise to warn family and friends so they won't be surprised when you scale back on outside activities and ask them to keep visits brief in the early days home.

But that doesn't mean you won't need your people. There are lots of ways that understanding family members and friends can support you while still allowing you time to bond. They can bring meals, help with laundry, clean the house, pick up the dry cleaning, take other kids to the library or soccer, or make a grocery run now and then.

You'll want to assemble some new resources as well. Talk with adoptive families in your area to get recommendations for good local therapists who specialize in adoption and attachment. In more remote areas, you may need to be prepared to drive awhile to get to someone who is experienced with adoption issues.

A good attachment therapist will have extensive experience working with attachment-challenged kids. He will work with the parent and child as a team, rather than separating them for therapy. His job is not to form an attachment with the child himself, but rather to help the child attach to the parent. To do this, the parent must be intimately involved with the therapy.

Therapists should be able to provide names and contact information of other adoptive families who've found them helpful. Call those numbers and chat with those folks. It is not uncommon for a family to try several therapists before finding one that fits their needs. It wouldn't hurt to schedule an introductory visit with a couple of different therapists in your area before your child gets home so you'll already have an idea of who might be a good fit for your family should you need some experienced guidance.

Also look into adoption support groups and cultural resources in your area. My area has a fairly active Korean community, as well as a number of families with Ethiopian kids. Ethiopian adoptive parents get together with members of the Ethiopian refugee community in our area a couple times a year for a picnic, complete with traditional Ethiopian food. This has been a great way for our kids to meet other adopted kids, as well as to get to know a few Ethiopian adults.

Preparing Your Home

I often use my nesting energy to prep meals ahead of time. A couple weeks' worth of meals in the freezer is a wonderful new-baby gift to give yourself. I try to freeze a bunch of casseroles. I also like to brown ground beef to freeze in meal-size portions, and cook and cube some chicken ahead of time. Precooked meat speeds meal prep tremendously. For more easy cooking ideas, you may enjoy the cookbook I wrote for busy families on a budget, *Family Feasts for $75 a Week*.

There are lots of ways to maximize space in your home to fit another child. Pinterest has some fabulous ideas for bunk beds.[3] A really good declutter can add several hundred square feet to any home. Get rid of furniture that's not serving a purpose.

Build shelving high in the garage to store out-of-season clothes, Christmas decor, and summer camping gear. The less you have to keep *in* the house, the bigger it will feel. I try to go through our house at least once a year and challenge myself to get rid of two or three garbage bags full of stuff from each room.

Think about where you might add built-in shelving. In one bedroom we built a bookshelf behind a bedroom door with shelves up to the ceiling, including a long top shelf that extends over a closet. It provides perfect high storage space for little-used toys, books, and stuffed animals, and uses only the tiny footprint of floor space behind the bedroom door.

Scale back your book collection. Chances are good that you're not reading most of them anyway. Ditto for your toy collection. (If you have a good way to convince kids to get rid of stuffed animals, let me know. I'm still looking for that magic bullet.)

Make sure your closets are well organized. Add shelving as needed. In our younger daughters' room we lowered a closet rod about a foot and added a second shelf above the rod. This rod makes it easier for short people to hang their own clothes, and the extra shelf above the rod is fairly easy to reach as well.

Shrink your clothing collection. Most people only wear twenty or thirty items on a regular basis anyway. Some larger families keep kids' clothes in the laundry room to make more play space in the kids' rooms. This also prevents little kids from pulling every item out of drawers to dress in the morning. (Or does that just happen at my house?) For more larger-family solutions, check out my book *A Sane Woman's Guide to Raising a Large Family*.

Melissa E. said, "We have six kids in our family, three bio girls and three boys adopted together. I remember bringing our boys home and how well the girls welcomed them. I remember thinking beforehand, *How will this affect our girls?* Somewhere along the way I realized that it was a bit selfish and one-dimensional of me to think that way. I am glad that I also started to consider, *How will this affect these three children who need parents?* And also, now I realize how making room and welcoming these three boys has decidedly affected our girls! For the better! Yes, it's been hard, but most of the truly good things we learn out of life are things we learn by struggling and are easily missed when we are never challenged to grow."

Preparing Your Other Children

Bringing a new child into a family where there are already children can feel like a big decision. However, most families find that if the parents are excited about the idea, the kids usually will be excited too. When we began the process to adopt our first son from Korea, our other four kids were between three and ten. We have some really precious video of the day the FedEx man brought us the first pictures of their new brother, with all the kids clustered around me as I opened the envelope, then all of us instantly exclaiming how cute he was. By the time Joshua finally came home, they were incredibly eager to hold him. Welcoming him was just the most natural thing in the world.

It wasn't always easy. He was fussy at first, and we invented what we jokingly called the "stations of Joshua"—a twist on the Catholic stations of the cross, ya know? He'd swing awhile, have floor time, get stroller rides around the house, play in the ExerSaucer, and I'd carry him in the baby carrier. Basically, we made a game of moving him from place to place and keeping him entertained. I changed diapers, fed him, and did the majority of the care. But our older kids had time each day when they helped. We all enjoyed him so much.

We were all surprised at the amount of attention he got. He was four months old when he came home, and cute, cute, cute. Our previous "baby," Daniel, also pretty darned cute, was nonplussed for a while by the attention shift. But overall he did really well with the adjustment. I'm sure all the kids had moments when they wished I wasn't so occupied with the baby, but they were all old enough to understand why it was necessary.

Nancy (www.indiatoappleton.blogspot.com) said, "For our first adoption, our sons were five and seven when their sister arrived home. She was one, so it seemed very much like welcoming a baby into the house. We did talk with them during the process about why some children need another family, but their developmental stages made these pretty simple conversations. Now we are nearing the end of a much-longer second adoption. Our daughter is seven, and our sons are eleven and thirteen. We've had more complex discussions about injustice (why poverty, death, or social stigma prevents women from keeping their children). They are difficult but good conversations—and allow our kids to see how God can create something beautiful out of suffering and pain. Our next daughter is two years old. As her homecoming gets closer, we are having family meetings to talk about orphanage behaviors, and we will check out materials and DVDs from the library that will help us all care for her. It's been so amazing to see our kids' compassion for their new sister—we can already see the heart of Christ growing in them as we wait for her."

Some siblings struggle more than our children did, especially at first. Teens can have some real reservations about adding another child to the mix, especially if their family is already large. I remember as a self-conscious teen hating the fact that my family was huge, and was devastated for a while when my mom told me that baby number eight was on the way.

In most cases being willing to listen to kids' concerns goes a long way toward bringing reluctant siblings around. Usually by the time new siblings arrive, kids are eager to welcome them. And the truth is, babies add a wonderful dimension to family life for older children. Yes, little ones get into your stuff and cause extra work. But there's nothing like that adoration of a baby to lift your spirits. Even a cranky teenager tends to melt when he's got a tiny sibling patting his face and hugging him.

Angela said, "We have one daughter adopted at age two. I've always felt that healthy, boisterous siblings are some of the greatest things we've had to offer foster and adopted children. I feel like the process has deepened our bio children's compassion and understanding of family."

Of course each new child does stretch parental resources a bit more. It's wise to talk with kids about the type of changes to expect, things like crying in the night and tired parents and needing to fit family activities between naps and feedings and other needs. Moms can also be less patient when they're sleep deprived. Reassure children that your feelings toward them will not change, even at times when you may be very preoccupied with caring for a new arrival.

Adopting older children introduces different stresses into a family. Families adopting children past infancy should talk to kids about grieving, bonding, and challenging behaviors that new children might exhibit. Dealing with the tough emotions of older kids can be just as draining and time consuming as rocking a tiny baby at night.

And as hard as it is to think about, make sure you talk with your other kids about what to do if a new sibling acts out sexually or threatens them physically. One of the reasons that many experts recommend not adopting out of birth order is because of the risk of predatory behaviors when adopting older children. It is impossible to know everything a child experienced before he came to you, and the very fact that he needs a family means he spent some time vulnerable and unprotected.

It is also wise to think about ways your other kids could get a break now and then in those first months with the adopted child. Though a newly arrived child may not be ready to go play at Grandma's for the afternoon, it may be just the ticket for kids who've always been with you, especially if there is a lot of stress and drama during those early months home.

Often time and attention is pulled away from the healthy kids to deal with the newly adopted ones. Well-attached kids do have more resources to deal with this, but that doesn't mean they are immune to the effects. Remember to spend time alone with them too. It's restorative both for you and your kids. And when you're feeling stretched thin trying to meet everyone's needs, remember God is their parent too. His power can multiply our every effort.

Beckey said, "We're still in the process of bringing our son home. Our bio kids are eight, five, and two, and we've involved them in the process from the time we started the paperwork for our home study. We've talked with them about the process and answered their questions (the main one being why we have to wait so long!). Our son has Down syndrome, so we've talked with them in age-appropriate terms about that and helped them meet other people with Down syndrome and see them in videos. Because his language skills will most likely take longer to develop, we have also been learning some sign language together. When new updates and pictures come, the kids all get a picture of him to print out and put where they would like. The older kids tend to carry it around in their pockets. Our five-year-old reminds us every time we pray to pray for his new brother."

Once, years ago, when I was worrying about how a new child would affect our other children, I was blessed to have a conversation with a wise momma of ten children. She reminded me that in a big family, there's truly a multiplication of resources. Big kids can get reading practice by reading storybooks to younger ones, and little kids in turn heap adoration on the older ones. Sure, they fight too—arbitrating squabbles is a normal part of motherhood. But there is a built-in system of support, whether they're teaching each other to play chess, or challenging each other to a race, or advising younger ones about driver's ed and college professors. There are times when teens are more receptive to wisdom from older siblings than parents.

The other day my eleven-year-old daughter, Emily, was remembering all the fun she and her now-teen brothers used to have together before they decided they were too mature to play with her. "Now they like to pick on me," she said matter-of-factly. "But they're helping me be tough. And I'm really looking forward to them being older. I think when they stop being teenagers they're going to be a lot of fun again."

Though her honesty made me wince—don't all of us mommas wish for those mythical siblings who never fight?—she has an amazingly long-range perspective for one so young. I also have great hope for their future relationship. By God's grace, this family that God has brought together from all over this globe will exist long after John and I have gone on to heaven, providing support and love and nurture to one another for generations to come.

Dana had this to say about the adjustment of her children to two new siblings:

"When my husband and I decided to go the foster/adopt route, my older kids were eight, eight, and seven. I was so worried about what the older kiddos would feel. My then-seven-year-old daughter was begging for a baby sister, so I wasn't too worried about her. When we received the call that there was a boy and girl twin set just released from the hospital, I was terrified of the adjustment, but my big kids took to it beautifully. Two years later and the shorties just about burst when the big kids get home from school, and they are the closest kids. It has been such a joy."

Growing Your Faith

The waiting time is tough for pre-adoptive families. Worries multiply. Doors are closed (or opened), and often plans morph in a way that parents couldn't have envisioned at first. But remember: God is in charge of it all, even the stuff we'd never be able to predict.

Make decisions with education and prayer and with the best wisdom available to you. But don't fear the unknown. God loves to set the lonely into families. He loves to supply all our needs. And He specializes in growing us in grace through adversity. Every time I come face-to-face with my own limitations, it leads me right where I should be in the first place: leaning on God's power, not my own. There's no better place to be.

It's amazing to me to look back and see the ways God orchestrated circumstances for our family. He put people in our lives who'd traveled similar paths before us and who could speak to our concerns or point out paths we hadn't yet considered. He never stopped encouraging. All along the way, we heard from Him, *Come along! This is a great adventure. It may be hard, but it's worth doing. Walk forward with confidence, knowing that I am right in the center of this.*

If you're looking to adopt as a way of growing your family, please know that you don't need a huge income or a big house or a hefty savings account, or even a bedroom for every single child. You do need faith in a faithful God who says that children are the heritage of the Lord. He loves to bring orphans into families.

A father to the fatherless, a defender of widows,
is God in his holy dwelling.
PSALM 68:5

CHAPTER 3

Building Heart Connections

Watching an attentive mother with her infant is a beautiful sight. The bright expressions and tone of voice that the mother uses. The way the baby tunes in to her momma, kicking her feet and moving her body in time with the mother's speaking and movement. The way the mother responds to her baby's expressions and vocalizations, instinctively noticing when the baby is ready for more lively play, or when she needs to quiet things down because the baby is getting overstimulated. A well-nurtured baby still cries, of course, when mom is unavailable or when discomfort makes it impossible for the mom to comfort the baby. But very often a tuned-in mom notices the baby's early signs of distress and responds before she even needs to reach a full cry. This beautiful synchronicity is something we often take for granted, but is essential to a baby's development.

Now picture a baby who spends his first months in a hospital or an orphanage environment. Different people take turns caring for him. There's no *one* familiar face and voice, no special person who takes the time to notice when he is getting tired or hungry. No one knows the child well enough to be aware of his unique temperament and needs. In fact, this baby may need to cry for a long time before a caregiver is able to respond. Then the response, even from a kind caregiver, is briskly businesslike, not warmly relational. Change the diaper, prop the bottle, move on to the next little squaller. The difference between these two types of care is profound, one that has long-term effects on a child's life. It is essential for us as adoptive parents to realize just how much a child loses when his early nurturing is not optimal, so that we can then move forward with wisdom and empathy to help our children heal from those early losses.

What Is Attachment?

This chapter, though heavy on theory and lighter on stories, is perhaps the most important chapter in this whole book. There are many, many great resources out there to explain attachment in great detail. But here in a few thousand words I'm going to give you a crash course, a brief synopsis of some of the best wisdom out there.

I strongly recommend that you also go to the appendix of this book and read the books I've recommended. The importance of attachment cannot be overemphasized, and the better you understand attachment issues, the more effectively you'll be able to parent. Attachment theory applies to children born to you *and* children adopted into your family, but kids who've been well nurtured since birth can be parented successfully in a broad variety of ways. Adopted children have experienced an early loss that narrows the range of good parenting options. Their needs are more acute and much more specific. We can't just pop an adopted child in a car seat, take him home, and treat him like a child who's had all his needs met well since birth.

The Attachment Cycle

A human baby is the most helpless creature you can imagine. Without care she would die. All she can do to signal her need is to cry. Crying is a baby's way of communicating that she is emotionally out of control (or dysregulated) and that she needs someone to step in and help her back toward calm (regulation), usually by soothing, feeding, or changing the environment in some other way.

Babies cry, and moms respond, leading them from dysregulation to regulation, over and over. In the first year of life alone, a parent will respond to a baby's needs thousands of times in thousands of ways. *Yes, I'll pick you up. Yes, I'll smile at you. Yes, I'll change you and feed you and rock you and make you more comfortable numerous times every day.*

Babies learn that feelings of happiness and satisfaction come from their mothers, and that they can trust her to meet their needs. Sensitive parenting helps babies gradually learn self-regulation. Even the sound of his mother coming will cause a baby to become calmer, to begin to soothe himself. That ability to self-soothe and self-regulate grows as the child does. Children who are responsively parented and have their needs met in infancy learn that they have a voice and that they have an effect on their world. Self-regulation is the foundation of mental health as an adult. And it all begins with the mother, in the first months and years of life.

The Attachment Spectrum

The effects of good attachment extend past childhood. We're all someplace on the attachment spectrum, and our attachment status profoundly affects our ability to respond to others. People often think of attachment as something that happens automatically between parents and children. In many cases this is true. But even with a mother and her biological child, attachment can take time to grow, and varying mixes of life stress and personality types can result in people living in various places on the attachment spectrum.

SECURE ◄──► ANXIOUS ◄──► AVOIDANT ◄──► DISORGANIZED

MOST HEALTHY ◄──► MOST DISTURBED

Secure Attachment

At the "securely attached" end of the spectrum, you'll find people who were parented responsively at critical points in their lives, or who because of resilient personality traits managed to get what they needed to be secure even in the midst of less-than-ideal life circumstances. A well-attached child enjoys Mom's company, seeks comfort from her in moments of stress, is glad when she returns, is easily comforted, and prefers his parents to others. His secure attachment makes him able to separate at age-appropriate times to explore the world. Because his parents have helped him modulate his emotions, he keeps trying when faced with adversity.

A cultural note here: many people in the Western world expect preschoolers to easily separate from their mothers for extended periods of time. Some little ones are ready. Some aren't. I passionately believe we shouldn't push our children to separate before they're ready, especially our little adoptees. They need their mommas.

The investment we make during those early years pays long-term dividends into their adult lives. A securely attached adult is able to have good relationships, is compassionate, and generally has good self-confidence and self-awareness. She's comfortable sharing feelings, has a well-developed intuition about other people and their feelings, and is able to make deep commitments as appropriate.

Insecure Anxious (Ambivalent) Attachment

Children develop anxious attachments in the face of unpredictable parenting. This can happen when parents have huge stresses or emotional issues in their lives that make them sometimes emotionally unavailable. This can also happen when a child has had multiple caregivers during infancy and childhood, is hospitalized for an extended period of time, loses a caregiver due to death, or doesn't have a chance to attach well to one person.

A child with anxious attachment is wary of strangers and is afraid when the parent leaves. Paradoxically, however, he isn't easily comforted by the parent. Lack of trust can cause him to be clingy, whiny, dependent, and demanding. An anxiously attached child also tends to be irritable and reactive, and often has temper tantrums. This is exactly the type of behavior our Ben was exhibiting as a toddler during his early months home.

Remember, it's attuned parenting that helps kids learn to self-regulate. Kids who miss that high-quality interaction don't self-regulate well. To add more relational difficulty, these kids often vacillate between trying to manipulate attentiveness from the parent and pushing the parent away when the parent is trying to be close. This makes them less gratifying to the parent, which can make more emotional distance between the parent and child, especially if the parent doesn't recognize it as a sign of relational difficulty and move closer to repair the relationship.

An adult who has experienced anxious attachment during childhood often exhibits this push-pull dynamic in love relationships. She is often reluctant to become close to others, worries often that her partner doesn't love her, pushes away when her loved one seeks greater intimacy, does lots of testing, and is devastated if a relationship ends. Often an anxiously attached person doesn't understand how her own insecurity contributes to relationship difficulty.

Insecure Avoidant Attachment

Children develop an avoidant attachment style when interactions with their caregivers don't go well and the development of trust is inhibited. This can happen when a parent is unreliable, absent, or rejecting. It can also happen when a child goes from one caregiver to another, even if both caregivers are good. Being nurtured is better than being neglected, obviously. But leaving a loving caregiver can be tremendously difficult for a child, and often makes it more difficult for a child to trust future caregivers.

These children avoid eye contact with parents and don't come to them for support in times of need. They're often more comfortable with the superficial friendliness of relating to strangers and acquaintances than they are interacting with parents and other important people in their lives. In fact, as they grow older, these children often take pride in not needing anyone, and rarely seek help when injured or disappointed, even at critical times when they could benefit greatly from nurturing.

Adults with avoidant attachment become more uncomfortable the closer a relationship grows. Since (consciously or unconsciously) they feel let down by important people in the past, they feel like they can only depend on themselves. They are often out of touch with their own emotions—it's too painful to go there. Because of this they are unable to share their own feelings, even in a close relationship, and find it difficult to understand the emotions of other people, sometimes even mocking deep emotions shown by others.

Disorganized Attachment

Children with disorganized attachment may at times show some features of all other categories. They alternate between clinging to and avoiding or fighting with the parent. They avoid eye contact and rock to self-soothe in times of stress. They may appear expressionless and are prone to destructive behavior toward themselves and others. They may hurt animals and often exhibit extreme issues with control. They have lots of self-doubt and feelings of *who would want me?* If left without help, these children can grow to become very disturbed adults. In less severe cases they are simply very inept at forming relationships and tend toward isolation and lack of trust.

The Effects of Separation

Children can show a mix of attachment styles at different times, but in general the more traumatic a child's life has been, the less likely he is to exhibit secure attachment. Dr. Karyn Purvis has a doctorate in developmental psychology and has spent a decade working with traumatized and abused children. She lists primary risk factors that are predictors of children from hard places.[1] These risk factors are: inadequate prenatal care or abnormal prenatal conditions, difficult or traumatic labor or birth, medical trauma early in life, abuse, neglect, and trauma.

Even a non-adopted child growing up with her biological mother can have her attachment status stressed by maternal depression and anxiety in pregnancy or after birth, prolonged daycare, or an extended hospitalization. An adopted child who has moved several times in infancy and childhood, who has experienced the loss of a first parent, or who has spent months or years in an orphanage is likely to have attachment challenges and will need years of steady, patient parenting to become well attached. Studies have shown that babies in orphanages only take a month or two to shut down and stop crying to signal their needs. It is wise to assume that *every* adopted child has wounds that will require attuned parenting to heal.

One rule of thumb is that a child will need to be with his adoptive parents for as long as he was away from them in order to begin to build good attachment. By that benchmark, a baby placed in his new family at twelve months of age might be well on his way to good attachment by his second birthday. A four-year-old might not feel truly secure until age eight. A ten-year-old may not become securely attached until adulthood.

Time lines like this may sound extreme. And some children do indeed overcome a difficult past more quickly. But building trust after relationship rupture takes time. Going into adoptive parenting expecting a long-term, attachment-building project is wiser than expecting a superglue bond within a month or two of homecoming.

Purvis went on to say: "There is much hope for these children and their parents. In our work we have yet to see a child that cannot experience dramatic levels of healing in response to the right approach and interventions focused on helping the child and parents develop deep and lasting connections."[2]

How's Your Attachment?

A factor that adoptive moms often overlook is their own attachment statuses. Every human on earth is somewhere on that attachment spectrum. Our own childhood experiences and tendencies will impact our abilities to connect with our children. Even adults who are functioning well in the world can be anxious or avoidant in times of stress. And here's the thing: parenting a child with less-than-optimal attachment experiences, as is the case with almost all adopted children, will almost certainly dig up more junk in you than you ever knew you had.

Many parents find that parenting troubled kids brings out the most fragile part of their own psyches. Being humble enough and self-aware enough to become aware of your own junk—we've all got it!—is a huge step toward sensitively parenting your adopted child.

Though I have a wise and kind mother, by the time I was nine years old, I had four younger siblings. My mom was understand-ably very busy with younger, needier people, and I learned to do a lot of things for myself. I never doubted my parents' love, and I took pride in being my mom's right hand. She and I have a great bond as adults. But I got used to being self-reliant as a child, to the point that it is still hard for me to ask others for help.

I also sometimes catch myself feeling irrationally frustrated by neediness in my children. I wonder if it subconsciously reminds me of the needy feelings that I pushed aside when my mom was busy with children who were needier than I.

How did my childhood affect my parenting? Well, I am effort-lessly nurturing toward my babies and toddlers. But once my kids reach the elementary years, I tend to step back. To a certain degree, that's natural. But too much emotional distance can leave a child feeling adrift on the ocean. In being so focused on the practicalities of life—"Did you finish your math yet?" "Go find your soccer shoes." "Put your clothes in the washer."—I know that I missed chances to interact on an emotional level with my now-grown kids.

I wish I'd been more adept at soul talk, at finding out what was really in their hearts. These days, as I learn and grow along with my younger ones, I'm making a conscious effort to check in more with my kids, to be present in their emotional lives. Sometimes I feel ham-handed and uncertain, like I'm tromping fragile soil with elephant feet. My children are not always willing to talk. But I'm getting better at reaching out and asking anyway. Thankfully it's also not too late to build deeper connections with my grown kids.

Your "junk" may look different from mine. But one thing is certain: our pasts *do* affect our ability to parent effectively, and to make real connections with our children—and with everyone else in our lives, including God. For our children's sakes, we need to be courageous enough and humble enough to look back and think through our own experiences.

Helping Children Feel Safe

Now that we've talked about the basics of attachment, it's time to think about how we can help our children connect with us. Often people think attachment is a warm, squeezy-hearted feeling. Really it is more like a dance. Central to this dance is trust. If you trust someone, it's easy to connect. If someone doesn't feel safe, you won't be able to connect with him or her in a healthy and meaningful way. Because of early wounds, many children won't be able to do their part of the relationship dance at first. Until kids learn to trust, we need to be emotionally prepared to reach out over and over without getting anything back.

It is completely possible for a child to *be* safe but not *feel* safe. And feeling safe is central in becoming attached. Newly arrived kids are watching and waiting for us to *ask* them into relationship, to show them we can be trusted with their hearts. Most adopted kids have known people who turned out not to be safe, either due to abuse or abandonment or inconsistent caregiving. How can we prove we're different?

Re-parenting

I didn't truly understand the huge importance of attachment parenting until I was parenting Ben, who'd spent half of his first year of life in a hospital bed, and then another year with a foster mom. Since he'd missed some of that early attuned nurturing, cuddling didn't feel comfortable to him. It took him months to learn how to snuggle his body in for a good cuddle. When carrying him on my hip, he would lean stiffly away, not grabbing on to me, and not letting his body lean on mine.

At first I assumed comfort would gradually come, but after he'd been home for months, I finally decided to literally coach him on how to hang on in the way that comes so instinctively to kids who've been with their moms since birth. I'd set him on my hip, place his little hands on the front and back of my shoulder, and show him how to lean toward me instead of away. It wasn't that he didn't want to do it—he truly didn't know how.

Shelly (www.yearn4surrender.blogspot.com) said, "In all the prep I did before our first adoption I never understood that

attachment is a two-way street. I was so focused on reading about helping our child attach to us that I never realized
how hard it would be to attach to my son. The process was
slow and long, and I was thankful for [support] groups to talk
about the issues, but I wished there had been more in print
about a parent's attachment journey. We get so wrapped up
in the photos and updates and the 'in love' feeling that we
think real love will come instantly. [An adoptive momma of
a large family] gave me the most wonderful wisdom on this
and it gave me such peace. She told me that it takes about
nine months in the womb and twenty minutes to attach with
a bio child and about nine months and twenty minutes to
attach to an adopted child. It makes sense."

Ben's resistance affected my feelings too. It's hard to describe
the physical tension you feel when holding an avoidant child. When
I look back and see his stiff awkwardness in some of the pictures
of our first year together, that feeling of heart tension floods me all
over again. When he became more comfortable with snuggling, I
felt such relief. And I think he did too.

It's impossible to understand how much heart connection happens subconsciously based on your child's response to you. The way
he clutches your hand when you offer it, laughs when you tickle
him, and seeks eye contact from across the room—all those tiny
responses encourage you toward more nurturing behavior, which
feels good to the child and encourages more warmth toward you. It
is an exceedingly powerful circle, one that validates you as a mother
in a primal, instinctive way.

When a wounded child pushes away even in tiny ways instead
of responding normally, it creates a tension, an off-balance feeling.

You know that something about the relationship isn't right, but unless you are very in tune and aware, you may not consciously note all the times your child leans away instead of toward you. The times his eyes slide away and avoid yours. When he doesn't smile back when you smile at him.

Don't take it personally; it's actually a function of your child's fear. It can be hard; we moms are wired to connect. A baby's normal responses validate us and help us feel like good mothers, so it affects our souls very deeply when connection doesn't happen naturally. We need to keep on mothering lovingly, reassuring our child he's safe, and trusting that God is at work in his heart and life, even when—especially when—there is little positive feedback at first.

> Renee and her husband (www.steppinheavenward.blogspot
> .com) adopted several babies and toddlers at different times:
> "At first I didn't feel I was doing anything well. The house was
> strewn with toys, dinner was thrown together, and trying to get
> a shower most days took more planning than a general and
> an invading army. I was nervous that I was doing something
> wrong and that the little ones were not going to love us or bond
> to us. I was pretty much a hot mess emotionally. If I had it to do
> over, I would worry less about the externals. I would simplify
> dinners, housework, outside activities and just enjoy the time
> with the little ones. I would not put so much pressure on [won-
> dering] if the child was bonded at that moment and just enjoy
> the process of bonding and getting to know one another."

Routine

So how do we help reduce that fear in our newly arrived children? Routine is one hugely important tool. If we can provide a predictable daily routine for our kids, we'll help them be better regulated. Traumatized children fear change. Anything that triggers a child's fear response will also trigger her fight-or-flight reflex. And that behavior ain't pretty, people. Warn kids of changes in routine. Acclimate them to new places. Prepare them for new experiences, and accompany them as much as possible. Follow through on promises.

Boundaries with Warmth

Sometimes when new kids arrive, we're so anxious for them to be happy that we provide zero boundaries for behavior. The problem is, boundaries help kids feel safe. We need to be calm, kind, and firm leaders. Communicate boundaries gently with smiling eyes and a sense of humor. Get down at the child's level, and speak simply and repetitively. Give children appropriate amounts of control over situations. "Would you like the red shirt or the blue one?" "Would you like to hold my hand or ride in the cart?" We'll talk about limit setting with various ages of children in greater depth in later chapters.

Accept Feelings

When kids' emotions flare up, remember to listen to and honor their emotions, even if their fear or anger seems unreasonable. Let them express themselves. Threats or rationalizing away feelings won't make fears go away, but letting them know you hear them will. Go with them into their pain. Repeat what they say so that you can make sure you hear it correctly. Even with older babies and toddlers, we can talk simply about the feelings they're expressing nonverbally, supplying them with the type of language they'll later be able to use to share their feelings.

Whole-Brain Parenting

One of the things that has tremendously helped with my understanding of the brain under stress is a book by Daniel Siegel called *The Whole-Brain Child* (see the recommended reading section in the back). It's a quick-to-read book that does a fabulous job explaining brain function in an understandable way. I can't recommend this book highly enough, whether you're parenting adopted kids or kids born to you, or just dealing with humans on a daily basis. The book explains the functions of the various parts of our brains and the way they work together. When humans are stressed and feeling threatened, we all tend to get dysregulated and go into downstairs-brains fight-or-flight functioning. Here's where lots of hot-headed decisions are made. Things that we don't mean fly out of our mouths, leaving us wondering later what possessed us.

Folks who are good at self-regulating can calm themselves and use their upstairs-thinking brain to return to the land of wise and thoughtful decision making. But self-regulation is learned from infancy via responsive parenting. Legions of people in the world, including many adopted kids, are not good at self-regulation. The more traumatic a child's early life has been, the more easily he tends to descend into dysregulation.

And—bad news—a dysregulated child can often drag down even a well-meaning and reasonably healthy parent. Robyn Gobbel, a social worker who specializes in adoption issues (www .gobbelcounseling.com), described what she calls trauma tornado.[3] For the sake of our kids, we need to be aware of when we're getting sucked in. If we go into downstairs-brain functioning right along with our kids, it's almost impossible to make wise parenting decisions. But the better we understand what's happening in our own heads, the more regulated we can stay ourselves, even if we're not always able to keep our kids regulated.

Attuned Parenting and Older Kids

When we bring home a child whose needs were not met early on, we need to nurture that child like a newborn to a certain degree, even if he or she is eight years old. We need to show the child that she has a voice in this new relationship, that her needs and wishes matter. Problem is, it's easy to say yes to an infant and harder to say yes to an eight-year-old who is testing boundaries. Always be on the lookout for ways to turn no into yes. Many times it can be done with a little creativity. Give a child a choice between two things, both of which you can be happy with. If you can't do it joyfully, don't bother. A child will pick up on an insincere or grudgingly given yes in a heartbeat, and the child will place more significance on the emotion you're showing than the actual yes.

In her book, *The Connected Child*, Dr. Karyn Purvis said that we should aim to say yes five times for every no. That's a lofty goal, isn't it? But here's why: when a child doesn't feel as though his needs are being met, it activates the sympathetic nervous system. His heart rate goes up. His blood pressure goes up. The more upset the child is, the more likely it is that his fight-or-flight brain will be activated, and the less well he can use his upstairs brain to cooperate. Kids whose needs were not met reliably in the past go much more quickly into that downstairs brain. And once they're there, children are much less likely to make good choices.[4]

When you meet a child's needs, it activates the parasympathetic nervous system, and that's where cooperation, learning, and healing can occur. An emotionally healthy child can be successfully parented in a variety of ways. But the more traumatized a child is, the narrower the range of parenting that will be effective.

The good news is that all kids can heal. But since trauma is relationally induced, it needs to be repaired within the context of a caring relationship. Therapists can guide parents to nurture their children in healing ways. Many adoptive families have been greatly helped by wise therapists.

It takes time, and challenging behaviors can feel very frustrating for a while. But children can't model positive behavior on the outside until their brains heal. Amy Monroe, from Empowered to Connect (empoweredtoconnect.org), said that expecting emotionally healthy behavior from an emotionally wounded child is like setting a three-month-old baby in the middle of the living room and telling him to walk to you. He's not mature enough to do it yet.

We parents desperately need to understand the level of woundedness that drives difficult behavior so that we can remain compassionate toward difficult behavior over the long term. We've got to address the root of the behavior instead of focusing on the behavior. Only then can we create a healing home.

Our goal as parents has to be helping this "baby" heal, whether she happens to be two or twelve, whether the healing takes six months or six years. Studies have shown that it can take three years of steady therapeutic parenting for the hippocampus to heal. (The hippocampus is the middle brain, and it is the regulator between lower-brain function and upper-brain function.) Yes, three years sounds like a long time. But the really great news is that the hippocampus grows until age twenty-five or thirty.[5] That means there's hope for every child.

Can I Really Do This?

If you're like me, you may be feeling intimidated by the weight of this chapter. Parenting wounded children is a huge task, but thankfully this isn't about perfect parenting. When we fail—because we will—that's our chance to model asking forgiveness and jumping back in to love again. By God's grace and mercy and power, we can go on to form rich and meaningful relationships with our children.

Healing will happen very quickly for some children and much more slowly for others. The battle belongs to the Lord. He knows we are all broken people living in a broken world. He is the real healer of every heart. He asks us only to be faithful.

He's put us together with our children for His glory, and sometimes that glory comes from walking step by step by weary step through great challenge. But the better we understand what's happening in our kids' heads—and in our own—the better we'll be able to help our children heal.

This is how God showed his love among
us: He sent his one and only Son
into the world that we might live through him.
This is love: not that we loved God,
but that he loved us and sent his Son as
an atoning sacrifice for our sins.
Dear friends, since God so loved us, we
also ought to love one another.

1 JOHN 4:9–11

CHAPTER 4

Helping Babies and Toddlers Settle In

It was January 2004, and there I was packing suitcases for a trip to Ethiopia. As I packed, I agonized. I worried. I prayed. We'd had such a tough time helping Benjamin settle in. This new little one, whom we were naming Emily, was going to be twenty months on homecoming, exactly the age Ben had been. And she looked somber and withdrawn in nearly every picture we had of her. I didn't want to go through the same type of trouble we'd had with Ben. Yes, he was worth every minute of it. But his first year home had been so very hard. Though I longed to love this little girl of ours, my heart quaked at the thought of working through that level of pain again.

But whenever worry won in my heart, my husband was my rock. "She's ours," he said, and there was a calm and complete certainty in his voice. His steadiness calmed me. I hoped that if

I handled those early days correctly, that if I did everything right this time around, maybe we'd get off to a good start. But all the while I feared that God was sending us toward an adventure that would be even harder than the last. Maybe harder than I could handle.

In February 2004, my thirteen-year-old daughter, Erika, and I got on the first of three planes on the thirty-hour trip to Ethiopia to get Emily. The closer we got, the more excited I became to see her. I prayed she'd fall in love with me.

She was living in a big Catholic orphanage in Addis Ababa, filled with kids of all ages sleeping two to a bed, around which bustled a bevy of cheerful nuns doing their energetic best amid the stench of poverty. On arriving at the orphanage, Erika and I were led through reeking halls, up stairs, past rooms full of infants, then into another room lined tight with cribs. My daughter was here somewhere, one of many little ones playing and sleeping and eating and crying and growing up within these walls.

In a minute I spotted her on the changing table in a frilly pink dress made for a four-year-old, a crunchy paper diaper, and sturdy high-top tennis shoes made for someone who had places to go. She was big, already a chubby thirty pounds—so much *not* a baby. The nuns set her on the floor, and I knelt in front of her, talking quietly, daring at first only to touch her hand gingerly. She pulled it back to her chest and stared at me with huge eyes, scared by the longing in mine.

I'd been waiting so long to get past the two-dimensional shots and begin to know the real person. But now that the moment had come, I wasn't sure how to go about this thing, this leaping into her life and taking her away from everything she knew. I got a toy and held it out until she was brave enough to snatch it. Then I gingerly rubbed her back while the nuns stood smiling and telling my baby loudly in Amharic that this was her mother.

Someone brought me a cookie with which to lure her, and suddenly I was the center of attention for every child in the room. I handed out cookies, and my daughter took one too, her eyes looking less wary. The nuns urged me to pick her up, but it seemed so abrupt that I took her by the hand and gently led her out of the room while she gnawed on her cookie.

It was then I realized that though she was nearly two, she was unsteady on her feet. So I finally did what I wanted to do from the very first second. I picked her up and held her close to me and kissed her cheek and smelled the unfamiliar smell of her. And she let me. Then suddenly I was carrying her away, moving toward this unknown adventure that was our lives. Together.

Rebecca said, "We had a fourteen-year-old son and a twenty-three-month-old son. Both knew we were adopting, but none of us knew when, where, or who, for that matter. When we received the call to go and pick up our baby girl in Texas, we had less than twelve hours to get ready, make arrangements, and get on the next available flight to meet our Grace. We knew the stay in Texas would be around a week. I was worried about leaving my youngest child because he had never been away from us for more than a few hours. A friend of mine told me to take the entire family. It was the best advice ever! My youngest didn't feel like we abandoned him and came back with a stranger. He loved the adventure of the plane ride and was so excited to see his new sister. My fourteen-year-old son enjoyed being in Houston, eating BBQ every night, and yes, meeting his baby sister as well. What was amazing and a blessing in disguise was how we all bonded. All five of us were cramped up in a motel room in Houston, Texas, waiting for the call that we could go home. That quiet time allowed us to simply bond with our newest member. There was no cooking, cleaning, school, or distractions. We simply played, rested, and enjoyed ourselves. We still talk about the adventure of the plane ride to get to our baby girl. God's hand was with us all. We absolutely cherish those memories together."

In the minibus on the way back to the hotel, she laid her head on my chest and fell asleep almost instantly. I snuggled in too, noticing the feel of her soft baby curls against my chin and thinking that back at the hotel a bath might be a good idea to wash off the orphanage smells.

At the hotel, she woke silently as we brought her inside. She allowed us to hold her. She ate the food we fed her. She clutched the toys we offered. But her entire demeanor was of silent watchfulness. She stayed where we set her, and her eyes followed us as we walked around the room. The only time she made a sound was at bedtime, when we turned off the lights, and I lay down next to her. Then she wailed and wailed. She didn't resist cuddling—in fact, she came into my embrace willingly. But it was obvious she was terrified. She cried for quite a while before she finally fell asleep in my arms.

The next morning, once awake, it was back to silence, with her sitting wherever she was placed and eating whatever we offered. For two days she watched us. We carried her around the hotel grounds, took her to breakfast, went shopping, went for pizza, played with her in the grassy courtyard at our doorway, fed her, changed her, and gave her baths. At night she cried in my arms before falling asleep.

Finally, on the third day after a bath, as she lay on the bed while I dried her and dressed her, Erika initiated a goofy game of peekaboo, hoping for a reaction. Emily smiled. As Erika redoubled her efforts, Emily laughed for the first time.

When I picked her up, she cuddled into me. It was exactly as if a shell had cracked away and there was her heart, open and ready for a momma. She fussed when I set her down on the chair and held out her arms to be picked up again. That night she snuggled tight into the curve of my body to sleep, as close to my heart as she could possibly be, and woke reaching for me if I rolled even an inch away in my sleep.

We got home, and it was more of the same. Once she decided we were good people, she embraced us with an open heart. She became a sparkly, delightful cuddle-bunny, totally unlike the sad-faced photos that so worried me earlier. For weeks I waited for the honeymoon to end. I took nothing about our relationship for granted, carrying her everywhere, feeding her bottles in the rocking chair, and sleeping with her at night. But it never, ever got hard. After all that worry, all that prayer, all my doubt, she was my miracle girl.

Melissa Fay Greene, mother of nine and author of *There Is No Me Without You*, used the analogy of a mobile when adjusting to the arrival of a new child. "I imagine a homely contraption of wire hangers and dangling threads with plastic dolls swinging at their ends; in times of tranquility, the mobile is balanced, the dolls turning lightly, as in a breeze.

Family-systems therapists also know that when a new child arrives, through birth or adoption, the family is thrown into disequilibrium: the power structure of the family, the parent and sibling relationships, the individual identities and roles, all go up for grabs. In the family-mobile metaphor, the same concepts are understood: when you tie on another doll, or two, especially when they are already the size of school-children or preteens, or maybe an already linked three-kid sibling group, or maybe a child who is cognitively or emotionally challenged, the thing goes haywire—the arms of the mobile tilt precariously, the threads tangle and knot, the figurines spin and crash together and some threaten to slip off. I imagine the sound our wind chime makes in the gales of a storm."

A certain degree of "storm" is unavoidable when a new child arrives, but there are ways to cope with the stress and to ease the transition for everyone. Infants often settle in to new families fairly well, especially with attentive attachment parenting. But that doesn't mean the job is easy, especially during the early months home when you're working hard to get to know each other. That's going to take time and energy—lots of it.

The most important thing to do at first with newly arrived babies and toddlers is to slow down, keep them close, respond attentively, and give yourself over to getting to know them. Keep expectations in other areas low. Set outside activities aside. Lower housekeeping standards. Later, life can move at a faster pace. Now is the time to build attachment.

One of the things that struck me on my visits both to Korea and Ethiopia is the way babies are constantly kept close to their moms. In Ethiopia, women go everywhere with babies on their backs, even while cooking and doing field work. In Korea, baby carrying is so much the norm that women's coats are sold in markets with zippered expansion panels so a baby can be worn in a carrier inside the mom's coat. And in both Ethiopia and Korea, babies sleep next to their mothers at night for years.

In the Western world, there's a decidedly different feeling. Sit in on a conversation with young mothers in America and chances are good that talk will soon turn to how well—or poorly—their babies are sleeping at night. The feeling seems to be that the sooner a baby sleeps in his own bed, the better. Moms of babies who don't sleep well want to know other moms' secrets for getting babies to sleep all night quickly. Moms whose babies do sleep well sometimes sound smug as they explain what they feel is the key to their success. And all too often moms who practice baby wearing and co-sleeping are told that they're spoiling their babies and fostering an unhealthy dependence.

This push toward independence is sad for any baby. After all, if you can't be babied during your first two years of life, when can you? But it is especially problematic for newly adopted infants and toddlers. In fact, it is exactly the opposite of what a newly arrived child needs to become well attached. Remember, you're trying to make up for time you missed together.

Amanda said, "If I had to do it over again, I would abandon any outside obligations and just do baby and family. I would hire help for the things that drove me crazy, like the house. I would order more pizza and eat more cereal for dinner and not have any company over or go anywhere. My expectations for myself at that time were ridiculous. Our son arrived on Halloween and we had out-of-town guests for Thanksgiving dinner (plus twenty guests!) and then we did a long-distance drive to visit family for Christmas. I had to go back to work in order to have the insurance our son needed three months after his arrival. I did hire a housekeeper at that time and that was the best decision I could have made. The thing I learned from this experience is that NOTHING is more important than your new baby. NOT ONE THING. And in order to care properly for your baby, you have to care properly for yourself. Rest is critical. Lower your expectations. Do much less. Pretend you DID just give birth and let your body recover. Just melt into getting to know your child."

Emily was pure joy to us. About a year after she came home, John and I started talking about a little sister for her. We wanted her to have a sister who was close to her age, and we knew that we didn't want her to be the only African American person in our family. It'd be hard enough to be living in "white" Idaho; we wanted her to have someone else in the family who looked like her. But we weren't quite sure about the timing. Adoption is expensive, after all.

We decided to wait until we had the money in savings, about $15,000. That's a lot of money, and we figured it would take awhile. We talked about ways we could live more frugally and upped our automatic payment into our savings account. We were also expecting a small tax refund, which we planned to add to the adoption fund when it came.

A couple months before that talk, in the fall of 2004, John had decided to sell a large, portable sawmill that he owned. For two months there were no calls. We were beginning to think it wouldn't sell. But *one* week after we agreed together to adopt when the money came, that sawmill sold. For $8,000. A few days later we did our taxes and learned we would be getting back $7,000, much more than we'd anticipated. Three weeks later we had an unbelievable $15,000 sitting in our savings account. We looked at each other and knew that God was saying, *Now*. We found out later that our daughter had entered the orphanage the very same week that John's sawmill sold.

We zipped through a home-study update and submitted our dossier to our agency in February. By April 2005, we had the referral of four-month-old baby Julianna. She had been born in the same area of Ethiopia as Emily, and was now being cared for at the very same orphanage in Addis. The final round of paperwork seemed to take a long time—oh, I wanted that baby in my arms! But just two months later we were flying to Ethiopia.

Since Emily had been home for such a short time, I wasn't willing to leave her for ten days. After much thought, we decided that I would take Emily with me to Ethiopia, and would bring our thirteen-year-old son, Jared, along to help me with both of the little girls on the way home. John would hold down the fort at home with the other five kids.

Walking onto the orphanage grounds with Emily and Jared, it felt like weeks, not months, since we'd last been there. Nuns and caregivers recognized Emily wherever we went, greeting her with happy kisses and exclaiming over how big she was.

Once in the baby room, I spotted Julianna almost immediately. She was fifteen pounds, not too tiny for a six-month-old. But her wobbly head and floppy little body made her feel like a much younger baby in my arms. Obviously she'd spent enough time in her crib that she hadn't really had a chance to develop much muscle tone. But she was bright eyed and curious, and didn't seem perturbed when it was time for us to walk out the door with her.

As we were leaving, we made a stop just down the hall in the room where Emily and I had our first moments together. I wasn't sure if she'd have any recollection of the place. She was barely three, after all, and it had been sixteen months since she had last been there. But as soon as we walked into the room, she pointed to one particular crib and said she'd shared it with a little boy who cried and made the bed wet.

It was a part of her story I'd never heard before, but that fact actually made the memory sound even more legitimate to me. It was a memory triggered by entering that room again. Thankfully she didn't seem disturbed by our visit. If anything, she was reassured by the warm kindness with which she was greeted by everyone. No, an orphanage is not an ideal place to live. But this one was obviously inhabited by kind and caring people, and by God's grace she had gotten what she needed.

Back at the guesthouse, we all snuggled on the couch to adore Julianna. Emily was overjoyed—she'd been looking forward to being a big sister. But I was glad Jared was there to help play with Emily as I cuddled Julianna and got to know her. Oh, it was delightful to be snuggling a tiny baby again. She was sweet and responsive right from the start, reaching up to touch my face as I held her bottle. I had hopes that her settling-in time might be almost as easy as Emily's. But I wasn't taking any chances. I planned to do everything I could to help her adjust well and begin the bonding process.

Helping Babies Settle In

Whatever your baby's age and life story before homecoming, there are several simple things that are wise to do to help make up for the time you've spent apart and to help build attachment. Carry your child on your hip or in a baby carrier at least an hour or so each day. A good, comfortable baby carrier will allow you to go for a walk, do a load of laundry, vacuum, or wash dishes while keeping the baby right there on your chest or back. For an infant or toddler under twenty-five pounds, a soft front pack usually works well: Ergobaby, Hug-A-Bub, and Moby Wrap are all excellent brands. I used a Hug-A-Bub for Julianna and loved how very comfortable it was for both of us, even as she grew.

Rock your child several times a day, in a rocking chair, on your lap, in a swing, or just swaying and dancing around the living room. Rhythmic motion is good for a baby's balance and eyesight, and is soothing as well. Some newly arrived babies feel uncomfortable with close tummy-to-tummy snuggles at first and may prefer to rock facing outward. Go slowly, and gradually acclimate him to cozy snuggles. Offering a bottle or sippy cup during rocking time often helps the baby accept closeness.

Be sure that you and dad are the main food providers in your baby's life for at least the first six to twelve months. Food is a powerful bonding agent, so don't hand that privilege off. Even self-feeding preschoolers can get little morsels from your hand now and then during a meal. Sometimes siblings or grandparents want to offer goodies, but for the sake of bonding it is really best if mom and dad are the primary source of bottles and treats.

Sleep with your baby. When our newly arrived children were infants, we'd often bring them into our bed with us at night. When Julianna came home, Emily was still sleeping with us, so for a while we had two kiddos in our bed. Some parents find that setting up a double mattress on the floor of the child's room is a good way to go. Even if you're not up for co-sleeping, you can lie down with your baby as she goes to sleep, then slip out once the child is asleep. If she awakens in the night and needs your presence again, it's easy and comfortable to go lie next to her again.

Play on the floor with your child several times every day. Play "This Little Piggie" or peekaboo. Roll a ball back and forth. Play chase. Make dolls talk to each other. Look at storybooks together. Build block towers and laugh together when your baby knocks them down. Laugh and be silly with your child every day. Tickle him. Dance with him. Be goofy and have fun! Laughter has tremendous bonding power.

All these activities are ones we tend to do naturally with little ones, but they're especially important for adopted babies who need extra time and interaction to make up for the time you missed before you became a family. And don't listen to the folks who say you're spoiling your baby. Spoiling is something that happens to fruit that is forgotten, not babies who are well loved. So love on that new kiddo of yours. It's one of the joys of parenthood, and it's just what he needs.

Signs of Challenge, Signs of Progress

Healthy attachment is a linchpin of all development. A baby who is not well attached to his mother will often have delays or challenges in other areas. Younger babies may have feeding issues that resolve once attachment is solidified. School-age kids may struggle academically until they feel secure in their family.

Ben had feeding problems at first. He gagged. He resisted being fed. He disliked many foods. I really wondered for a while if he had some sensory/texture issues with food. But lo and behold, once we got past those first difficult months and he began to feel more secure with us, his food issues gradually went away. Body, soul, and spirit are inescapably entwined. When his spirit began to heal, he became able to accept physical nourishment from me as well.

Sometimes it is obvious that a baby is doing well in your care and is moving toward a healthy attachment. It all just feels right. But other times it can be difficult to tell. If you're feeling head over heels in love with this new arrival, that's a great sign. But keep in mind that it often takes mothers awhile to fall in love, even in the case of a baby born to you. And in the case of adoption, it can take months. So don't panic if it takes you some time to feel in love.

Shana is mom to three children by birth and two from Ethiopia, one adopted as an infant, the other as a teen. "Somewhere in the first couple of months [with the infant] I realized that everything I had read, and everything I had done, was to make sure the baby was attached to me. I had never worried about whether I would attach to the baby. As I was driving down the road one day, I realized that I was going through the motions of being a mother to my son, but that I didn't feel like his mom. I felt like a complete failure as a mother. After all, what kind of person wouldn't fall head-over-heels in love with a squishy, adorable, helpless little baby? A few weeks later I was talking with a girlfriend (who didn't know how I was feeling) who mentioned to me that when she gave birth to her second-born, she was surprised to discover that she didn't have an instant connection with her. Yes, she loved her, and yes, she was glad to be her mother, but nothing compared to the way she already felt about her first-born. This was a mom I looked up to. This was a woman who I knew adored her children. Hearing her confession was so freeing to me. I no longer felt like I was the only one who had ever felt that way. And suddenly I had hope. Quietly, my mantra became 'fake it until it's real.' And that's what I did. I held my baby. I fed him. I kissed him. I bathed him and rubbed lotion on him and smiled at him and cooed at him and did all the things mommies do with their babies. Slowly but surely, I felt my connection with my son grow. I loved him from the beginning, but now I was starting to fall in love with him. Looking back, I wish I'd sought more help. I wish we had done some sort of counseling from the start. I wish I hadn't assumed that attaching to a new baby would be instant. Five and a half years later, I am completely in love with my son, and couldn't imagine our lives without him. But those first few months were a lot harder than I had imagined."

Moms also sometimes suffer from post-adoption depression (see chapter 10), which can complicate your feelings. Especially if you are feeling depressed, don't use your emotions as the be-all, end-all gauge of your child's adjustment. But in general, if you feel as though your child is responding well to your overtures, you are enjoying your interaction with your child, and you can see growth in your relationship, you are probably moving toward good attachment. By the time Julianna had been home a couple of months, it became obvious to us that she was settling in well and not having trouble with attachment. Oh, we were all in love!

Here are a few assessment questions you can ask yourself if you're wondering how your child is doing with attachment:

How's the eye contact? Watch your child's eyes. Does she make good eye contact with you, or do her eyes skitter away from yours when you try to meet her eyes? Does she look for you when you are across the room and seem to want you to notice what she's doing? Does she look into your eyes when you're feeding her a bottle? Sometimes eye contact is awhile in coming, so don't worry if it doesn't seem to be there in the first month or so. Playful games like peekaboo are a great way to help your baby gradually become more comfortable with eye contact. But babies who make good eye contact are actively seeking connection, and that's a wonderful sign.

How does your child's body feel in your arms? Your baby's body language can help reveal his emotional state. Does he mold his body into yours when you hold him? Does his body remain rigid in your arms? Does he flop away? Will he allow you to hold him close, tummy to tummy, when he is getting his bottle, or does he twist away? Does he clutch your shoulder with one or both hands when you carry him on your hip? Is he open to affection when it is initiated by you, or does he seem to prefer it just on his own terms?

If you have a baby who is resistant to being held, try using a baby carrier as you go about your day. The fact that you are occupied with your work even as you carry the child sometimes feels less threatening, less focused, and provokes less resistance. And yet he's still getting the body contact and becoming acclimated to being touched.

Whom does she prefer? Does your baby prefer you, or does she happily go to anyone? Often folks misinterpret a child's comfort with strangers and extended family as a sign of security. But if that behavior is not paired up with *appropriate behavior toward mom*, it's actually a huge warning sign. Unattached babies are indiscriminate. In fact, they often actively try to charm the socks off every stranger in sight while also pushing away mom for all they're worth.

Moms often feel as though their kids are hunting for a better mom. Sometimes kids also have a marked preference for dad for a while. That mom relationship is often scary for kids at first.

Once your child's attachment becomes more secure, your baby will probably begin to shy away from friendly people at the grocery store or fuss when others want to hold her. Grandma may be sad when that happens, but in terms of attachment, preferring mom over anyone else is an excellent sign. Keep in mind that some children are naturally sociable. But if you as mom get the vibe that your child would happily go to Timbuktu with the mailman without a backward glance, that's a sign that a strong attachment hasn't happened yet.

Does he seek you out when he is hurt? If your baby seeks you out when he is in distress and accepts your soothing, that's an excellent sign. He's seeing you as a safe place and is feeling comforted in your presence. Kids who struggle with attachment often seem to want to control the interaction, to accept affection only when they ask for it. If you feel a lot of push-pull and your child is showing signs that he's trying to control all your interactions, make sure your interactions are very nurturing. If the power struggle seems to continue, you'd probably be wise to get some counseling, both for yourself and for your child.

Keep in mind that for most babies, progress is uneven. During times of stress, your baby may regress to a level of neediness that you haven't seen in months—or he may go back to resisting affection to a degree that you haven't seen in a long time. Be aware of your child's cues, but don't be afraid to shower your child with extra affection during times of struggle and regression.

Kids need to be *dependent* before they can learn independence, and an adopted child is often not going to look the same developmentally as a child who has always been with a nurturing mom.

Kids adopted past the newborn period often have needs that seem unusual for their chronological ages. Some will act much younger than their ages and will struggle with anxiety. Others will tend toward inappropriate independence.

The answer in both cases is to amp up the nurturing. Rock, cuddle, and offer sweet treats. Sugar is a great bonding agent! Stay close and parent responsively. There will be folks who don't understand this amped-up nurturing—they'll think you're going to create a kid who never matures. Don't get sucked in to that fear. Being mothered with high nurture is exactly what will best help children eventually gain maturity.

Hang in there. Helping a child attach takes months or years, not days or weeks. A child who tended toward independence may get clingier as she begins to heal. The more you are able to see her neediness as a good sign, as a sign that she is drawn to you, the easier it will be for you to respond with the patient, warmhearted love that she needs to become completely secure eventually.

After the challenges with Ben, we felt very fortunate that Emily and Julianna settled in quickly. They were snuggly and responsive little kiddos who within just a few weeks of coming home were looking to me for everything, and who didn't seem to have any major delays. Within two months of coming home, Julianna had developed good muscle tone and strong legs, and she crawled and walked at normal times.

And Emily repeatedly amazed us with her quick mastery of English. When she had been home seven months, while cuddling with me at nap time, she said to me in her brand-new baby English, "Thank you, Mommy. Thank you, happy, me." She came to me with an open little heart, fell in love with me immediately, and never let go. I know now what a gift from God that is.

I still wonder how children can respond to the same momma so very differently. I suspect that Emily had excellent nurturing in her first year—enough to carry her through those long months in the orphanage. Joshua and Julianna were home with us by the age of six months. In contrast, Ben's seven months in the hospital, followed by a year with a foster mom, left him feeling traumatized and distrustful at first. Personality may play a factor as well. It seems logical that it might be harder for an introverted child to move between families. And coming home at a young age is no guarantee; there are plenty of adoptees who come home in young infancy and still struggle.

We'll never know for sure all of why the adjustment was harder for some of our kids than for others. We do know, however, that we are tremendously grateful for all our children, both the ones who survived rough starts to settle in quickly and well, and the ones whose hurts required extra help and time to feel safe and begin to receive our love. God is good, all the time, and His grace and goodness is all over all our stories.

You will be secure, because there is hope;
you will look about you and take your rest in safety.
JOB 11:18

CHAPTER 5

Bringing Home Preschoolers
and Older Children

In March 2007, John and I began to tentatively talk and pray about adopting again, maybe a sibling group this time. We were thinking that two little boys under the age of seven would be a good fit for us. Our youngest was only two, so we thought we'd wait at least another year, and since I'm a baby lover through and through, I was hoping again for a baby.

Over spring break, I was looking at pictures from an orphanage on a blog post written by a friend who'd just returned home from Ethiopia with two new daughters. One older girl's picture reached out to me and grabbed me in a visceral way. It was crazy, but I felt like I was looking at my own daughter.

I e-mailed the friend and asked about her. She was eleven, didn't have an adoptive family yet, and also had a nine-year-old sister. Both were delightful, he said. In fact, he wished he and his wife could adopt them, but they were already moving forward to adopt two of their friends.

I brought the girls' pictures to John, my heart moved but fully expecting him to tell me I was nuts. Hey, *I* thought I was nuts. We'd been talking about adopting two little boys under age seven, and here I was bringing him photos of two girls who were over eight. You can't get any more opposite than that. But instead of telling me I was nuts, John looked at their pictures, read the description that my friend had written, and looked at the pictures again. "I wonder what their story is," he said thoughtfully.

We began to talk, and almost immediately to imagine how they might fit in to our family. Better, maybe, than starting again with babies when we already had so many older ones. Our oldest daughter, Amanda, was nineteen at the time.

We prayed. We e-mailed our agency for more of their story. With each small discussion and step forward, peace grew in us both. The polar opposite of our first angst-filled adoption decision, it truly was the peace that transcends all understanding. God was on the move in both our hearts, unmistakably reassuring us that this was the way we should go.

Within a couple of weeks, we were moving full speed ahead with home study number five. As we walked forward on faith, doors opened. Within days of committing to the girls, a long-awaited book advance arrived in the mail, providing half the money. An adoption benefit from John's employer would cover $4,000 more on homecoming. The adoption tax credit would reimburse most of the rest of the $26,000 cost the following year. Our social worker roared through our home study in record time. Our fingerprints were quickly approved, and by mid-May, a mere six weeks after we first spotted the girls, our dossier was on its way to Ethiopia.

That week we got devastating news. The Ethiopian government had changed rules and would no longer allow families with
more than five kids to adopt. We worried that this might not work
after all. After a few days of uncertainty while the agency got more
details, we learned that the ruling would only affect families whose
dossiers arrived in Ethiopia after a certain date. Ours had arrived
in Ethiopia just days ahead of that deadline. We hadn't known how
important it was to get our dossier off in time. But God had, and
had orchestrated everything. To us it was more evidence that God
wanted the girls with us.

While we waited for paperwork to process, we filled a welcome
bag with clothes and pictures of our family that another adoptive
family delivered to them. To help the girls imagine themselves
in their new home, we printed, cut out, and laminated a life-size
poster of them, then took pictures of the poster in various places
around the house: at the dining table, on our front porch, and on
their beds in their bedroom. We were already imagining them with
us, and we wanted them to see that vision too.

Letters also flew back and forth between us as we waited. One
letter from them contained a paper-bead necklace to me from the
older sister, Lidya. Her first gift to her new momma. I was touched
and wore it almost nonstop for the next year as a symbol of the
hope we all felt at this new beginning.

In July, John and I went to Ethiopia together to get the girls. It
was the most surreal thing, walking through that care center looking at faces, trying to spot our girls. Kids ran ahead to find Lidya,
age eleven, and when she came out of her classroom, she and I were
crying and hugging instantly. Zeytuna, nine, was reserved when I
hugged her, but smiled shyly. We toured the orphanage and met the
girls' friends. When it was time to go, Lidya asked to spend one last

night at the orphanage with friends. While John and I were trying to decide what to say, Zeytuna quickly said no, Lidya should come with us. Maybe she was afraid of being alone with us, but at the time I took it as a declaration: we were a family now. We followed Zeytuna's lead and gently told Lidya that she would be coming with us.

The first days together in the guesthouse we were careful, smiling strangers, everyone on their best behavior, trying so hard to please one another that we said yes to almost anything they asked. We taught the girls to play Uno. We let them use the camcorder. We bought them treats, clothing, and much-needed shoes at the markets. We let them eat whatever they wanted at mealtime and spent time at the orphanage so they could spend a few last precious hours with the many friends they'd made. We were trying hard to show them we were good people, and that they could be happy with us. The girls were also obviously eager to please, agreeing easily to any suggestions we made.

On the plane ride home, zapped by stress and jet lag, they slept and slept and slept. At our home airport, greeting their new siblings, they were dazed and exhausted. In the van on the drive home, the radio played a song about the mansion our Father is preparing for us in heaven, and my heart leaped.

The song perfectly symbolized what we were so longing to give the girls: a comfortable home and a loving family to love them and meet their needs. Their eyes were wide when we walked in the door. I watched them looking around our comfortable living room, and all I could think was, *Please, God, let them be happy.*

In the early days at home, acutely conscious that they were adjusting to a whole new world, we led them with gentle, pantomimed suggestions. The twenty shared words that we had between us made communication challenging. If they didn't seem to understand a request, we'd usually drop the issue. That first month home it felt like we were babysitting someone else's kids: slightly uneasy, everyone smiling and on best behavior, but thankfully relatively conflict-free.

Two months home, the shine was wearing off. The girls were discovering that their new home wasn't paradise. They enjoyed picking and eating garden produce, especially plums from our prolific plum tree. But they were deeply suspicious of most of the food I served. They were disappointed that we didn't watch much TV. And they didn't understand why we insisted that they gather around Dad with the other kids for stories at bedtime. Deeper yet, whether or not any of us truly realized it at that point, the girls were also beginning to realize that the hurt from their past didn't just evaporate when they arrived in their new family.

We knew the changes in their lives had been huge, so we tried to stay chill and keep expectations low. But our big kids were beginning to be irritated that the new kids were getting away with so much—"They only have to eat rolls and bananas, Mom?"—and our little kids were beginning to imitate the pouting of the new girls and ask for similar exemptions from food they didn't like. Yikes.

We knew we were being inconsistent and began to feel that to be fair we needed to hold all the children to the same standards. But our first attempts at limit setting sent the girls' budding discontent into full bloom. Where had their pushover parents gone?

Showers and Clothes and Hair

Battles came on every front. At first when the girls refused to shower, I waited it out. *Major in the majors*, I told myself over and over, keeping my smile firmly in place. Except the same sweaty clothing, worn in layers day and night, would show up for days on end. In August. Along about September, I'd had enough, and walked them together into the bathroom with new clothing and a command to shower and wash their hair. I offered to help with hair washing, but they refused. And glory be—once they realized I was serious about it, showering became a regular thing. Maybe I should have insisted sooner.

My first attempts at hair braiding didn't go all that well either. Zeytuna was okay with letting either me or Lidya braid her hair. But Lidya's curls were so thick and abundant that they challenged my unskilled hands. My first cornrows were so bad that she spent the next two months flatly refusing to let me touch her hair. Puff ponytails, French braids, and head scarves were things she could do herself, and so she did. But I learned from Lidya and practiced on the other girls. One day after I'd given Zeytuna an excellent braid job, Lidya decided I was enough improved to offer me her head. Occasionally. If she was in the right mood, and if I asked with just the right humility. Alrighty then.

It was incredibly hard to decide which battle was worth fighting and which wasn't. I prayed so often for wisdom. When one of the girls decided one Sunday that she wasn't going to church, running into her room and slamming the door, John followed her, unlocked the door, picked her up matter-of-factly, walked out to the garage, and set her into the van. And we went to church, ready or not.

Years later I realized her action that day may have actually been terror at the thought of interacting with a mob of strange kids in Sunday school while possessing only a few dozen words of English. At the time we thought it was rebellion, but thinking back I wish we'd found a way to be gentler that day.

Clothing for church was another issue. We've always had all

our girls wear skirts or nice slacks to church as a sign of respect, but the new girls wanted to go super casual. As experienced parents, we were not eager to change our family rules midstream. Looking back, it may have been more kind to compromise on Sunday clothing. But the big kids already thought we were overindulging the new girls. And my momma heart wanted them to look like Ostyns, not orphans, especially on Sundays. (I know—pride, right?)

I took the girls shopping several times, hoping to find dresses and skirts they'd actually enjoy. But still, every Sunday they'd come out in holey jeans and ratty T-shirts, seemingly determined to look like no one cared about them. I finally decided that to decrease Sunday-morning stress, the clothing discussion had to happen on Saturday evening. Each week I'd pick two or three options and tell them to choose one. They still lobbied for other options, which I was willing to discuss as long as it involved a skirt or nice pants. But moving the discussion to Saturday evenings greatly decreased the Sunday-morning chaos.

The Sunday clothing battle was just one of the many challenges we faced in those early months. Oh, it was hard at first, for all of us. What I remember most about those first months is an underlying feeling of tension in my chest. They were strangers to me for a good long time—strangers whom I desperately wanted to please and to live in harmony with. It was hugely draining to parent them in a way that allowed them latitude and grace but that was also congruent with the mom I'd spent twenty years thoughtfully becoming.

I have a vivid memory of working at the kitchen counter with the girls one day. My husband came home from work and greeted me with a smile. On the surface we all looked tranquil and happy, but inside I was an exhausted, depleted mess. I was fooling everyone. But all I could think was that no one, not even John, knew how hard this was, to shoe-horn two precious strangers into our home and be a family.

The newness jangled me at every turn. I was trying so hard to be a nurturing, happy momma. I smiled until my cheeks hurt. But the girls didn't feel familiar to me, and I didn't feel familiar to them either. Kids who've been in a family since infancy already know all the tiny unspoken rules of a family, little stuff like asking before turning on the TV or grabbing a snack, and bigger things like going to church as a family on Sunday.

Cultural differences added to the challenge. Ethiopian kids are taught not to look adults in the eye; Americans show respect by making eye contact. A single upward tilt of the chin means yes in Ethiopia—but to my American eyes, it looked like pugnacious belligerence. Over and over that chin tilt would trigger a flare of frustration in me before I even had the chance to remind myself that meant yes.

In Ethiopia, toilet paper goes in the trash, not the toilet, to avoid plugging weak plumbing. And folks wash their own underwear in the shower, not in the communal laundry. Some things (like eye contact) remained a battleground for years. Other things were resolved easily: once the girls understood what was normal in America, they were happy to flush TP and hand off their undergarments to the washing machine. But each issue was just another reminder of how little we knew one another.

By the time they'd been home three months, the honeymoon was officially over. The girls still didn't like my cooking. They preferred TV over reading and multiplication—what kid doesn't?—and dug in their heels when I insisted on schoolwork. When Zeytuna didn't want to do her chores, she foisted them off on Lidya, who'd spent years being her caregiver and took over without a whisper of complaint. Sometimes I didn't even notice that Lidya had once again stepped in and rescued her. When I explained to Lidya that Zeytuna needed to learn to work too and asked her to stop helping, Lidya was angry. They'd been family long before I came into the picture. What right did I have to legislate their relationship?

Where's the School Bus?

Homeschooling was another hard adjustment. In Ethiopia, they'd been some of the privileged few who actually got to go to school. Now here they were in America, the land of opportunity, stuck in a homeschooling family. I tried to remember the huge changes in their lives—how hard it must be to move to a whole new world and get used to a new family. But the constant arguing and disrespect and sullenness over phonics and clothes and food and everything else under the sun left me worn down, with my sympathy threadbare.

Six months after they came home from Ethiopia, we were at a breaking point. The girls were still grieving terribly, and that grief was coming out as the most amazing stubbornness I've ever witnessed—and I'm pretty stubborn myself. The girls didn't want to please me. Frankly, they didn't even like me. In moments of anger they'd yell that I wasn't their mom, that I would never be, and that signing papers didn't make it so.

I'd gone into this expecting that the first months would be hard, but I really expected life would be getting easier by the six-month mark. Instead, six months in, our home life felt intolerable. I couldn't make anyone happy. I went to my doctor for an antidepressant that turned out to make my feelings even more miserable and chaotic. Maybe some other medication would have worked, but after one horrible week on meds, I wouldn't risk drugs.

At one point John and I went to see a family counselor, who ended up knowing less about adoption and attachment issues than we did. The session ended with him scribbling down the names of books *we* recommended to *him*. Nice for him, but a $185 fail for us. More investigating revealed that the nearest counselor skilled in adoption issues was in Portland, a seven-hour drive, completely impossible on our budget and with our other children. John was adamant that we not take on debt for expensive counselors, especially since both girls had already told us they wouldn't say a word if we brought them in for therapy.

So we prayed. Oh, how we prayed. Yes, we were limited by funds, by availability of therapists, and by medication that didn't seem to work. We were exhausted trying to love and wisely parent these girls who seemed to hate us. But still we believed we had a God who was mighty to save. He had brought us here, and we hung on to the hope that amid all our limitations He still had a good plan for our future.

I'm convinced it was God who led my husband to a temporary plan to ease life that winter. Homeschooling had become an endless battle for the girls and me. Seeing that it wasn't working, John sat me down and told me I wasn't teaching the girls anymore. At least not for a while. For one whole semester he took over the girls' education. He has a flexible schedule that allows him to work only three days a week, and on his days off he brought the girls out to his workshop and taught them school while he worked.

On the days he worked away from home, he set assignments out for the girls—things like handwriting and computer learning games and educational DVDs that they could mostly do on their own. I supervised the girls when John was away at work and gave them new projects as needed, but for an entire semester I basically did not teach them. My husband saw what I didn't: at that point in our lives, as they settled in to our new family, I could not be their teacher. I just needed to be their mom. And frankly, that was hard enough.

Other families in that situation have sent kids to public school for a while. We were tempted, and truthfully we'd *all* have welcomed the break. But their lack of English and current emotional fragility made us doubt they were ready for such a venture. Also, home-schooling is at the core of our family culture, and we fondly hoped that more time together would eventually allow better bonding. But for a while I had to let go of my ideal vision of homeschooling.

Did it work? Yes. The girls were more respectful toward John. They learned their multiplication facts and practiced phonics. I taught the other kids in the morning, then greeted the girls when they came indoors at lunchtime and spent the rest of the day just being mom. All of us were better off for a few hours of separation. The next fall I stepped back in to the teacher role when our relationships improved. But I'm really grateful to my husband for recognizing we needed a different plan for a while.

Though we ended up sticking it out with homeschooling, many families (even ones who had planned to homeschool) decide that a better plan for them is to send kids to school. Mothering newly arrived older children can be a tremendously draining job. And often it feels much more doable when parents and kids have a regular break from one another. Flexibility is a huge virtue in cases like this. You need to be willing to try different things and do what works for your unique family.

Jamie of www.afamilieslove.com brought home siblings that were two and four on homecoming:

"Biggest thing I learned: it takes almost as many years for them to acclimate as they lived in their birth country. [That was a] huge revelation for me! No matter how well they are doing in English, expect them to understand a lot less than they appear to understand, for several years. Stick to concrete concepts, even if they seem to understand more, and use as few words as possible. Sleep next to them/near them for as long as you can. It may be the only time they relax with you for a while, and it will foster a close relationship, plus you will be close by for those late at night, darkness inducing tears/questions. Allow them to be little, babyish even, for a while. They had to be 'big kids' and responsible for a long time, well before they would have here in the US, so give them their babyhood/pre-K childhood back. If you can keep them home for a year, homeschool them; even if it is hard, and you may not want to be together, do it anyway. Tell them daily that God has a plan for their lives here, He is working His will in their lives, and your own, and He is doing a good work in them, through them."

Learning English

I think one of the reasons that homeschooling was such a struggle at first was that I so much wanted to help the girls catch up to their peers. I thought that if I was organized and intentional, within a year or two they'd be working at grade level. I've learned since then that becoming fluent in a second language takes four to ten years on average. And while immigrant kids are learning English, their peers who have always spoken English are *also* learning new vocabulary words at a regular rate. It is unlikely that an English as a Second Language student will truly catch up to their peers when it comes to vocabulary.

Our girls did catch up in math within three years. Now as teens, they're doing well at algebra and geometry. But since they spent a decade immersed in another language, spelling and grammar are still challenging. I am encouraging lots of reading and lots of dictionary use when words are unknown, and they have made amazing strides. But these days I have a better grasp of how huge a job it is to learn a new language.

Another thing I didn't understand at first was that learning happens best when kids aren't stressed, and when they feel secure in the love of their parents. Newly arrived kids are under huge stress and haven't had time yet to form attachments. It can be months or even years before a child feels safe enough and relaxed enough to focus on learning. In my eagerness to help the girls make up for lost time, I expected too much, too soon.

Karen Sear, adoptive mother and adoption psychotherapist, wrote, "I remember that if it's this hard for me to change and learn new ways, when I really, really want to (and I am a fairly mature, well-balanced adult with tons of coping strategies), how much harder it must be for my kids to change and learn, even when they really, really want to. It's enough to bring me to my knees."

These days, when folks ask me about homeschooling and new arrivals, I advise them not to begin formal school until their kids have been home a year. Instead, focus on helping the kids feel safe.

Talk with them. Play games. Cook and do housework together. Show them how family relationships work and what it looks like to be a daughter or a son in your home. After a year, I'd add tiny bits of schooling in very short spells, no more than one to three hours a day for the first couple of years. Always, always focus most on relationship.

A gradual phase-in can work for kids in public school too. Some kids are raring to leap in to school when they've been home a month, and some families' work situations make full-day school necessary right away. But if you have the luxury of choice, there's a lot to be said for taking a few months to get to know one another, with half-days of school for perhaps another three months, working into full days after the child gains language and seems ready.

It can be easy to worry that a child will fall further behind if you don't leap into school full bore, but the better attached the child is, the better he will be able to learn in the long run. So don't be afraid to begin by investing in relationship. Meet their needs for safety and attachment first, and math will come in time. Reasonably motivated kids can learn what they need when they're ready. I came across a study recently that found it is possible for a child to learn all elementary school math in only twenty contact hours.[1]

Remember also to focus on kids' nonacademic strengths. Maybe it's good people skills or athletic ability or a good work ethic or a great sense of humor or mad hair-braiding skills. Maybe they're passionate about music or art or the inner workings of machines. Notice and nurture those skills and interests. This helps kids approach life with a feeling of self-confidence instead of the vague feeling that they don't measure up.

Nurture and the Power of Routines

For a child to bond, two things are essential: low anxiety and a high level of closeness. While waiting for our children to come home, we often develop a long list of things we want to do with them. But we've got to remember our biggest aim first—to help them feel safe. Remember, kids can *be* safe without *feeling* safe. *Feeling* safe is essential for trust to grow. So we've always got to work on building their 'felt safety'. The more we can keep kids tucked close to us, and the calmer and steadier we can be, the safer they're going to feel.

It feels natural to nurture tiny ones. But older kids need us close too, whether they realize it or not. In fact, the kids who most resist that closeness are the ones who need it most. At first our girls had a hard time settling in and enjoying bedtime stories. I'm sure it was partly the language barrier, but it was also discomfort with the intimacy of family time. Eventually they got more comfortable with it, and it came to feel normal, but at first it was really hard for them to sit through.

Play Together

Floor time is just as good for big kids as it is for preschoolers. Legos, board games, and puzzles are all great ways to bond. Sometimes it can be challenging to find games that everyone can play, but it's worth the effort to persist. Kids who've experienced trauma miss out on chances to play, so help them catch up. Show your child that your family takes time for fun. Sometimes I have to coax my kids to play games with me, but usually they end up enjoying them once we get started.

Talk

As you go through the day, speak simply to your child, explaining what you're doing and what is going to happen next. Explain things even if you think she understands what you are doing. Use gestures to make your meaning clear. This richly expressive speech will help your child learn language more quickly, as well as show her more about what you are thinking and feeling. Ask questions about emotions. Be aware that kids from hard places often cannot sort their emotions especially well. They may deny emotions at first, be unwilling to share, or truly be unable to name the jumble of feelings that exist within them. Here are some of the soul words we use sometimes to talk about our feelings at our house: glad, pleased, scared, panicked, furious, grouchy, isolated, embarrassed, shocked. You can find a more comprehensive list at www .howwelove.com/wp-content/uploads/2012/05/SoulWordList.pdf. This is very much a work in progress, but my hope is that talking about feelings routinely will gradually help my family get more in touch with what's going on inside them.

Touch

Hug and kiss your children right from the start, even if it feels awkward. If your kids are uneasy with touch at first, go gently. Try shoulder bumps, high fives, and quick side hugs in the beginning. Pat their back or touch an arm as you walk past. Be matter-of-fact, and be aware that some kids won't reciprocate for a good long while. Establishing a habit of touch will accustom children to receiving and eventually giving affection.

Work Together

Although it is good to wait on school for a while, draw your child in to normal family work right from the start. Work side by side so that it feels like a group project and not slave labor. An older child can fold towels while you fold clothes. A younger one can pick up his blocks while you dust in the same room. When you're making dinner, a child can rip lettuce or peel carrots.

Kids who help in the home gain a feeling of competence and know they're contributing members of the family. Some folks hesitate to have their kids help at first. But working together feels different than setting the child to a task and walking out of the room. And waiting to start the "normal" routine until after the newness has worn off can leave kids thinking work is punishment instead of a normal part of family life.

When our daughters were newly arrived, I worked hard to keep the routine as predictable as possible. We sang songs after breakfast every morning, straightened the house together after school each day, watched a video most afternoons—a welcome hour of downtime for all of us!—and played games and read stories at bedtime. The girls learned quickly that Friday night was soccer in the park with friends and Sunday morning was church.

Don't go overboard with TV. It's easier than relationship, you see, and can cheat kids out of valuable interaction time. Some adoption experts recommend that newly arrived children not watch TV at all in their first six months home. For families who send their kids to school all day, that's wise advice. For our homeschool together-all-day clan, I found that an hour of TV time (with captions turned on) was a good break from the intensity of relationship building. We all loved that low-stress part of the day during their first year or two home.

Handling Holidays

When waiting for our daughters to come home, I looked forward to sharing the wonder of Christmas with them. But our first low-stress Christmas didn't happen till they'd been home for four years. Holidays are a break in routine, something traumatized kids often find very stressful. Many kids also have emotion-laden memories of Christmas with their first families. Birthdays and Mother's Day can also be hard, especially for older children who remember their first families.

That first Christmas after our girls came home, one of our girls spent quite a long time making paper garlands to decorate the house, just as she had with her first mom. She and John also spent hours hanging Christmas lights all over the outside of our house. In fact, she coaxed John into the biggest holiday-light display we'd ever done. I was so glad to see these little signs that she was trying to embrace her new life.

But Christmas itself was hard. We had lots of little meltdowns, lots of moments where the day seemed not to be living up to their expectations. Looking back, I think that the anticipation of that first Christmas buoyed them up for weeks. And I'm sure they desperately missed their first mom. Afterward they both seemed to fall off a cliff emotionally, and their funk was much deeper than the January blahs that hit so many of us after Christmas.

Experts say it is wise to keep holidays very low-key at first. Celebrate closer to home than usual. Keep routines as normal as possible. It can be challenging to balance everyone's needs, especially if there are other children in the family. Holiday routines are usually much loved, and it can be hard to curtail the whole family's holiday celebration for the sake of the newest arrival. But doing too much with a newly arrived child can cause more stress than anyone wants.

Especially that first year or two, be willing to compromise. Maybe you'd never want to skip Christmas Day church and your family gift-opening time. But it might be okay to go to Grandma's only for dessert. You may be tempted to host a party at your home, since that would keep your child in a familiar setting. But remember that preparing for a party takes lots of time. In the long run it might be less disruptive to have the party at Aunt Sue's and just stay for an hour or two. Tell extended family that you're on maternity leave and that someone else needs to host the big shindig.

Think about scaling back a little in your prep for the holiday too. Maybe you can send a New Year's letter instead of a Christmas letter. Or just skip the letter this year. If baking stresses you, buy your Christmas cookies. Use gift bags instead of gift wrap. Think of what will give you more time on the floor playing with your precious new arrival. Another year you can get back to your regular ways of celebrating.

Fear, Limits, and Expectations

When you're struggling to love your child well, take some time to sit quietly and think about some of your child's hardest moments in life. Did your child spend time as an infant in an orphanage? Did she experience abuse? Did he stand by a parent's grave? Really inhabit that hurt with your child. Go to this painful place as often as you need to, to keep that compassion at the forefront. It is an enormous thing we ask kids to do, ripping them away from their entire lives and asking them to grow happily in a new place. Some plants transplant easily. Others struggle. It is true for children as well.

It doesn't mean you can't guide and teach your child about right behavior, but compassion gives greater power to our interactions. Kids can tell if our hearts hold love or anger. Assume that most of your child's difficult behaviors stem from fear of losing control over his life again. And in the case of an immature child, those attempts at control may make zero sense, and may feel to the parent simply like rebellion.

Also remember that kids who miss out on months or years of family time are often *years* younger emotionally than their chronological age. Often parts of a child's psyche get stuck at the age they were when they suffered their greatest loss. A behavior that can feel ridiculously immature from a thirteen-year-old may be much easier to handle if you recognize the scared little six-year-old still stuck behind those thirteen-year-old eyes.

Acknowledging our child's trauma and immaturity does not mean ignoring disrespect and disobedience. Newly arrived kids often have a few days or weeks of a honeymoon period, when they're too unsure of their situation to test boundaries, but soon enough you'll need to acquaint your child with the limits in your home. The most important thing to remember about this is that every interaction with a wounded child needs to be within the context of connection. They need to have a voice. They need to feel safe.

In *The Connected Child*, Dr. Karyn Purvis described the ideal parenting approach as high structure, high nurture. If you focus *first* on the child's need for safety and connection, Purvis said you can usually get the child to go with you. Even a fearful child longs, deep down, for a relationship with the parent. And in times of stress, when emotion runs high, don't be surprised to see that little six-year-old still grieving her momma.

Keep your words simple and your expectations moderate. Think in terms of giving kids experiences that they didn't get at a younger age. Rock and snuggle, and give frequent snacks. Warm, sweet drinks are very nurturing. Kids will often regress during times of stress, illness, or big changes in the family. Be aware of the little cues that they may need a bit of extra nurturing. One of my daughters won't tell me when she's sick, adamantly denying illness even in the midst of a raging fever. I'll notice she is more quarrelsome and put my hand on her forehead to confirm what her mood helped me guess—that she's sick and needs a bit more fussing over.

In times of stress, even a teen can be pulled next to you on the couch for a bit of a chat. The key is to keep it playful and to be sensitive to their signals. I sometimes couch it as "I need a hug . . ." When kids are rude or cranky, sometimes I will give them the "consequence" of five kisses or ten hugs. They groan, but they also usually end up laughing. And any correction that ends up with more closeness and better connection is a success.

Support Sibling Relationships

If there is a very volatile child in the home who sometimes hurts others, often after an incident it is tempting to first address the offender. It's probably better, though, to first comfort the one who has been wounded. Sometimes we also may need to put restrictions on a child's activities to keep other children safe. For example, the one who sometimes hurts others may need to sit on a chair near you during school hours so that you can closely supervise. I also usually give the offender a chance to make restitution for the hurt, either by redoing the interaction with kindness or by doing a chore for the wounded sibling.

Even positive interactions between siblings can sometimes feel problematic to a tired momma's heart, especially if children are using interaction with each other as an excuse to ignore parents. One of our daughters can be talking and laughing happily with her brother, then turn instantly stone-faced when I call her name. I felt repetitively hurt by that behavior. After feeling stuck in my resentment for a while, I realized that I needed to reframe the way I was thinking about the issue.

Here is a family member with whom my precious girl has bonded. That's wonderful for her heart! Lord willing, they'll have years of being brother and sister even after I've gone to heaven. That realization allowed me to respond totally differently the next time he got a smile and I got a frown. Instead of growling, I gave her a quick hug and said to her brother, "Good job helping her smile. She needs to smile more. It's good for her."

She shot me a peevish look and muttered that she actually smiles all the time. I answered mildly, "Awesome, it does good stuff for your brain." Then I went back to what we were talking about. That little comment didn't turn her attitude around. In fact, for the moment she quit smiling at her brother and went back to being sullen with me.

But that's not where the victory was. The victory was in my head. I'd been able to stay relaxed and warm, and to acknowledge her good relationship with her brother. And to be honest, that bond is something she and I both cherish. Anytime we can reframe a frustration in a more positive way, we're going to feel calmer and more successful overall.

Building Trust

Kids who are with nurturing parents from birth naturally learn to trust their parents. Children who come to a new family have no reason at first to trust that their new parents have good intentions for them. Most older-adopted kids have experienced abandonment by or death of caregivers. Some have been abused by primary or interim caregivers. Those early experiences make them afraid to trust. What if they're let down again?

Kids may need years of consistent, loving care before they begin to trust, and they may resist trusting even in the face of much love and care from new parents. I found out after years of school-time unhappiness that one of my daughters thought I cared about her schoolwork only because I wanted her to get out of the house and never come back. No wonder so many talks about school were going badly.

I decided to begin explaining my motivations very deliberately: "I took you to the movie today (bought you this shirt / gave you this ice cream) because I love you." "I'm helping you with reading because I want you to have skills to learn whatever you need to learn later." "I'm talking to you about your feelings because I want to help you have a happy future."

It felt mechanical, but it wasn't automatic knowledge for some of my kids. And it's been helping. Recently my daughter's cell phone was getting low on minutes, and though I'd told her she was in charge of buying minutes herself (as her older siblings had also done), I impulsively bought her some just to surprise her. Her brother asked why, and before I could answer, she grinned and said, "Because she loves me." Yes!

What About Lying?

One behavior very common to newly arrived children is lying. This can be hugely frustrating to parents, who understandably want to stop it as soon as possible. However, we've got to remember that lying comes from fear. In fact, all sorts of crazy behaviors come from fear. Backing the child into a corner and forcing him to admit his lie only makes the fear—and the lying—worse.

Instead, we need to meet that fear with nurture. It may be totally counter to what you're inclined to do—it can be really aggravating to have a child lie to you, and it seems as though the child should be punished. But punishment is *not* going to extinguish this behavior. Only when a child feels safe will he stop lying.

If you have a child who lies, first of all, don't put her in a situation where she feels like she needs to lie. Don't ask who broke the vase. Say, "I bet you were really scared when that happened." If she counters with the lie again, gently remind her you love her and she can tell you the truth.

It's okay to offer natural consequences for dishonesty. A child who has shown he can't be trusted may need to stay closer to mom for a while. But don't get too hung up on forcing him to tell the truth. Too often that creates a stand-off where no one wins. It's enough to talk about the importance of telling the truth and then offer increased nurture.

Months down the road, after you see evidence that trust has begun to grow, it is okay to address an obvious lie with, "Would you like to try that again?" Wait until your child has calmed down, though, and keep your words gentle and your face loving. Praise him if he tells you the truth. Reassure him if he doesn't—eventually he will be strong enough to tell the truth.

Always, when lying pops up, redouble the nurturing activities. This is about fear. Treat the child as if she is much younger. Remind her over and over that she is safe. Keep her close, keep activities to a minimum, and keep the daily routine predictable. Rock, hug, and interact playfully. Let him know very clearly that his mom can meet his needs.

It takes time, lots of it. It takes the Holy Spirit at work in your own life, because it is not easy to set aside old ideas of punishment and justice and fairness. You will be learning and growing through this just as much as your child. Remember how much you have been forgiven in your own life. Pray, seek the guidance of the Holy Spirit, and love your child like crazy. Reassure that fearful heart, and gradually he will begin to trust. And when that happens, it will become much easier for him also to tell the truth.

Renee (www.steppinheavenward.blogspot.com) brought home six children via adoption. She said, "I believe the best piece of advice I received was from a friend who had adopted four older children, two from disruptions. She told me to always seek to set the children up for success. For younger children this meant keeping them very close by so I could help learn to play and interact with their siblings and to be safe. I found with our older children this may mean finding an outlet for their talents to balance out the struggle of learning English and schoolwork.

"We connected by spending time together and getting to know one another. I felt such an urgency to connect and I wanted attachment to happen instantaneously, but all relationships take time. I would encourage adoptive parents not to place that weight upon themselves or their children. I would encourage them not to look at every circumstance as an attachment issue, but to enjoy them in the good moments and realize in the hard moments that bad times and struggles are also a part of bonding. It doesn't feel as good, but it's true.

"I wish I would have known that [the parenting] marathon is run mile by mile. I think so many times I was worrying about mile twenty-five when we were at mile one. I would have loved to have someone come alongside and say, 'You are doing great. Your stride for this part of the race is perfect. You handled that obstacle really well.' It would have saved me a lot of wasted mental time and energy, and I could have just slowed down and enjoyed or persevered through the mile I was in."

Finding the Strength to Keep on Keeping On

If you're reading this and are beginning to feel overwhelmed at the tremendous amount of effort this all seems to take, you're not alone. Shepherding a newly arrived older child is very challenging work. For some families, their intense efforts begin to pay off within a year. But it is more common for an older-adopted child to take thoughtful, intensive nurturing for three to five years, or even longer.

It is equally common for the mother to need some time to truly fall in love with her new child. One mom who adopted many kids said, "If you go into an adoption with a feeling of commitment and you can wait patiently, the love develops. I don't expect the child to be an instant son or daughter and love me unconditionally, and I don't expect that from myself."

During that settling-in time, however long it takes, remember to nurture yourself as you nurture your child. Get enough sleep. Eat good food. Exercise. Your own emotional stability will help to steady your child's moods. If you find your mood slipping, even though you are taking good care of yourself, don't hesitate to seek counseling or look into getting an antidepressant. You need to care for yourself to be able to help your child.

Karen Sear wrote, "The most surprising thing to me was not realizing what attachment truly meant. I had read books, but they were always told from the 'how to get your child to attach to you' perspective. My kids attached fairly quickly. It took me much, much longer. At some point in my journey somebody had told me, 'Fake it till you feel it.' Sounds a little distant, but I embraced it. When I was at the end of my rope, I was determined that my child would have fun and feel a part of my family even if I was not as attached to them as they were to me. A friend reminded me once that about three months into our adoption I said to her, 'I feel like I'm babysitting and I'm just waiting for their mom to come get them.' I still can't believe I said that out loud.

"The greatest thing I've ever done as a mom is realize that I needed to change. I needed to radically alter my perceptions of what was important and attend to the needs of my children. It took me awhile, maybe three years to fully attach. Understand, I had that tiger mom thing immediately. It was 'mess with my kids and I will cut you' type tiger love. But I distinctly remember [later on] watching a movie and looking down to find my son draped over me like a large lap dog. I hadn't even known he was there. It had felt so natural. Up to that point I'd always had an awareness of where he was in relation to me."

Signs of Progress

As attachment begins to grow, here are some things you will begin to notice with your child. He'll begin to seek you out and want to be near you. He'll begin to feel more comfortable with affection being offered by you. Eye contact—sometimes sketchy at first—will begin to improve. He may show off for you, and check in when you are across the room from each other.

I still remember the first time I noticed one of my older girls "checking in" with me visually when we were away from home. I'd signed the girls up for swimming lessons and was sitting reading a book nearby. I was looking up often to see how things were going and realized my younger daughter was keeping an eye on me too. Oh, what a wonderful feeling that was. We still had a long way to go attachment-wise, but it was tremendously meaningful to me to notice that she was keeping an eye on me.

One thing I've had to learn over and over again along this journey, though, is that I can't look to my children for affirmation. Even good parenting is going to feel ineffective sometimes when you're parenting kids from hard places. The outcome of their lives is up to God. My job is simply to be faithful day by day—not perfect, just faithful—even if I don't always see progress.

Another thing that has surprised me along this adoption journey is the way God is working on my own heart issues even as I work to win my children's hearts. In giving me this task that sometimes feels impossible, He's chipping away at my self-sufficiency and teaching me to lean on His all-sufficient grace. In asking me to love children who don't always love me back, He's illuminating His *perfect* love for a very imperfect me. I began this journey longing to be a blessing and a change agent in my children's lives. I didn't expect that my life would be equally changed. Through adoptive motherhood, Jesus is refining me like gold. I am confident that He who began a good work in *all of us* will carry it on to completion until the day that He returns to bring us with Him to heaven.

Now to him who is able to do immeasurably
more than all we ask or imagine,
according to his power that is at work within us, to him
be glory in the church and in Christ Jesus throughout
all generations, for ever and ever! Amen.
EPHESIANS 3:20–21

CHAPTER 6

Sleeping and Eating and Date Nights, Oh My!

OUR YOUNGEST DAUGHTER, JULIANNA, STILL LAUGHS when she tells the story of being ousted from our bed by Dad when she was five years old. "I kicked Daddy in the night so much, and then he said from now on I had to sleep in my own bed."

By that time she was only sleeping with us for the early-morning hours. The move to her own bed was not traumatic, and she knew that if she was afraid in the night, she could still come to us for a hug and a tuck-in back into her own bed if needed.

Being the youngest, she actually spent more time in our bed than any of the other kids. But our attachment-based response to our kids' night needs began back in our early days of parenting our biological kids. In general, we tended to do whatever it took to get everyone as much sleep as possible at night, which meant that all of our babies and toddlers slept with us for a while. Attachment parenting turned out to be a good fit for our adopted children as well, especially in their first months at home.

I know that many parents subscribe to cry-it-out methods of sleep training. They may work for some babies, and believe me, I have vast sympathy for the level of exhaustion that makes parents desperate to get children sleeping better. But I'm convinced that the cry-it-out method of sleep training is a risky thing for newly arrived adopted children.

Children's needs don't just quit at bedtime. In fact, night is often the most terrifying time of the day for newly arrived children. We can prove ourselves trustworthy by responding to our children's cries at night. Having ten kids, I completely understand how difficult this can be. More than once in the midst of bone-weary tiredness, I've thought how convenient it'd be if kids came with an "off" switch (to be used only at bedtime, of course!). But I suspect that one of the reasons God didn't do that is He knew it'd be too tempting to overuse it.

There are lots of theories floating around in the world about how to get babies to sleep. In the case of a baby who's been with his mom since birth and has had good, steady nurturing, a wide range of options can work. But here's the problem with sleep theories and adopted babies: unless your baby was placed in your arms straight from birth, you don't know what kind of nurturing he's received. He's already had several caregivers, and he's had experiences that you probably aren't aware of. And even babies placed in your arms at birth can be negatively affected by extra stress hormones that circulate in a mom's body during a stressful pregnancy.

It takes months, sometimes years, for a child to become well bonded to new parents, and it takes months for parents to really learn and understand their children and recognize signs of distress.

Some kids are whiny and hard to console when distressed. Many others are hyperalert and disturbed even by small changes in their environments. Still others shut down and appear very quiet and unresponsive although their hearts may be racing with fear when you lay a hand on their chests.

I look back now at pictures of my children when they'd just arrived, and I can see the stress all over their little faces. Could I see it back then? No! I didn't know them well enough yet. It took months for me to be able to reliably read their faces.

Because of that newness, I think it is wisest for adoptive parents to plan on continuing with attachment parenting right into the night hours, even if it means missing sleep. Babies cry to express needs. Newly arrived babies are going through a huge adjustment. If your child had time in an orphanage, he most likely cried at times without having his needs met. Now he's in a new place with new people. It's got to be scary. Every cry in the night is a chance to teach your child that you are there for him. You care. He is no longer an orphan. Now he has a momma.

Of course we *eventually* want kids to learn self-soothing techniques. But here's the thing: healthy babies learn self-soothing only *after* experiencing parental soothing. For your baby's well-being, that first year or two at home needs to be about nurturing and bonding. And when it comes to bonding, nighttime is prime time.

When my babies wake at night, I respond in the lowest-key way possible that will still meet their needs. Some little ones are reassured by a few minutes of patting on the back. Some go right back to sleep when they're brought into our bed. Others need a bottle or some rocking/walking for a few minutes to settle down.

Sometimes I'll go lie in the recliner in the living room with the baby, but I try to keep the scenery boring—no TV, low light, etc.

I want my child to feel sleepy, not entertained. If you need something to occupy your head and make night waking easier, you could use earbuds to listen to a book on an MP3 player. Some parents find that bouncing on an exercise ball with the baby helps him get back to sleep. Whatever approach works for you, the important thing is to be there for him.

In the wee hours, when exhaustion feels overwhelming, we all wonder if responding really is the right thing. That's when I remind myself that even if this little one is *not* a newborn, he's relatively new to our family, and crying is the way he communicates.

When babies are waking frequently, I try to keep things as simple as possible. I keep bottles and diaper-changing supplies in a basket next to the bed, and make sure to have a dim lamp nearby so I can change diapers without turning on the overhead light. Nightgowns or sleep sacks make night diaper changing much quicker and easier.

Rest During the Day

When you're responding to frequent night needs, it's essential to rest a little each day yourself. It is always tempting to use nap time to get things done, but if you are sleep deprived, it is really better to get some rest. Even lying down for twenty minutes in the afternoon with your feet up and your eyes closed is restorative to your body. Yes, even if you don't sleep, and even if you're lying on the couch with *Sesame Street* playing for your three-year-old. If you also have preschoolers, consider getting high door locks on the front and back doors so you don't have to worry about your three-year-old opening the front door and letting the UPS man in. That's no way to wake up from a nap, let me tell you.

Fresh Air and Chocolate

When babies are waking you often at night, you sometimes go through a day in a fog of exhaustion. A brisk walk outside every day, even for fifteen minutes or so, can get your blood flowing and help you regain a more positive outlook on life. Stick the baby in the carrier and the toddler in the wagon, and everyone will benefit from the outing.

I firmly believe chocolate also has medicinal qualities, especially for tired mommas. I routinely stockpile chocolate in hidey-holes around my house, to be used on desperate days when a mood lift is essential. Try it. You just might like it. Even if you need to exercise again afterward.

Sleep Training and Orphanage Babies

Babies who spent any time in an orphanage have already experienced crying without being responded to. I'd rather have a baby who knows I will respond than a good sleeper. Why? Because a baby who trusts me is a baby who is becoming attached. Attachment is the glue that binds humans together, makes interaction fun and enjoyable, and is the basis for all future interaction in life, including—yes—those tough teen years. If that means less sleep for me for a few months now, so be it.

This belief does not come from a position of naive inexperience. We had several kids who slept extremely poorly at night. Josh woke up every sixty to ninety minutes for five months straight, day and night. He was a hyperaware child—still is—and he slept very lightly. I woke many mornings sure I could not carry on until bedtime. And yet somehow through God's grace, with a bit of help from chocolate and coffee, I survived until the end of the day. Every day. God is gracious.

I had days during that time where I doubted the wisdom of attachment parenting. I even tried the cry-it-out method with Josh for about a week. He screamed, red-faced and utterly hysterical. For hours. And hours. Maybe if I'd held out just a little longer, he'd have given up. Maybe. Knowing him now at fifteen, I'd guess not. He is *the* most determined kid I've ever known. Thankfully, I don't think I scarred him too much by letting him cry. But wow, was I miserable listening to him. A week of crying it out did absolutely zippo for his sleep habits.

What really made me give up on the cry-it-out approach was the way it tore at my heart. We mommas are wired to respond to our babies' cries. Letting my babies cry made me miserable, whether I was standing outside the door, lying in bed with a pillow over my head, or taking a brisk walk around the block while my husband held down the fort at home. Even when I was bone-tired, when I responded I felt a sense of rightness, like I was a good mom. The only way I could let my babies cry even for a short time was to harden my heart to their misery. How healthy is that for a momma trying to get attached to a new baby? I would argue, not at all.

Aside from what it might do to a momma, there's the baby's trauma. Penelope Leach, a British psychologist, did studies that measured stress hormones in babies who were allowed to cry. She found that a stress hormone called cortisol went sky high. Leach said, "What you're doing at this stage is sculpting the connections in the brain. When someone comes and comforts the baby, the cortisol gives place to the happy hormones, endorphins, which flood in instead. So over time, if the baby is almost always picked up and comforted, then the connections in the brain will teach it that when stress hormones flood the brain, endorphins kick in."[1]

Eventually the stress hormone/endorphin connection becomes strong enough that during the second year of life, healthy babies begin to be able to self-soothe. Babies who are not comforted during infancy miss out on the chance to develop that brain connection between cortisol and endorphins, and may always find it hard to self-soothe, even into adulthood. Adopted kiddos who were not soothed well as infants due to extended orphanage life or a less-than-ideal start for other reasons may not be good at soothing and calming themselves even into adulthood.

I'm not writing any of this to lay guilt on anyone. We're all doing the best we can on this parenting journey. But the research seems to suggest that it is best to respond to kids whenever possible. Some babies will not suffer harm from extended crying. But human beings vary tremendously in what they are able to withstand emotionally, and we don't come to adoption immediately understanding everything about our babies. And—this is just a momma observation based on my ten kids—the babies who are most likely to fray their parents around the edges at night are almost always the ones who are *least* able to tolerate the stress of being alone at night. Their cries are communicating hints about their temperaments. They exhaust us because they truly are *more needy*.

Certainly, we all know adults who are easily bruised by life, who experience more pain and need more reassurance when the bumps and thumps of life happen. There are babies with these same personality needs. It is at best naive and at worst downright unkind to refuse to respond to needs simply because they come at an inconvenient hour of the day.

Keep in mind also that some infants seem to adjust well, but still have trouble bonding. One friend said her son was an easy baby who seemed to adapt well to multiple caregivers while she worked. But as a toddler his behavior became very challenging. Around the age of four they realized he was actually struggling with anxiety related to attachment issues. Several years of intensive attachment parenting allowed him to eventually become well attached to his parents, but my friend wishes she'd been aware of the importance of attachment parenting from the start.

Gentle Sleep Training

John and I were mostly in agreement about how to respond to our babies at night. But there were times when one of us would want to respond quickly and the other would say, "Wait, let him cry a minute, and let's just see if he'll go back to sleep." Tired parents in the wee hours can have volatile moments of disagreement! But because we had made a general rule to respond at night, our arguments were infrequent, and in general we found we all slept best by simply responding at night. However, different parents have different needs and comfort levels and can sometimes come to different conclusions. And even those of us comfortable with responding at night wish our kids would sleep better. What to do?

If you're desperate from lack of sleep and want to *do something* to help your babies into better sleeping patterns, there's a wonderful book called *The No-Cry Sleep Solution* by Elizabeth Pantley. Pantley incorporated some aspects of active child training with a really nice sensitivity toward a child's needs. Her book is not specifically geared toward adopted kids, but her suggestions jive very well with expert recommendations for adopted children while still giving parents a certain level of control over the sleep situation. Here are some ideas:

- Make sure your baby gets plenty to eat during the day. If he's less hungry at night, he's less likely to wake at night.
- Establish a regular nap schedule as much as possible. A consistent daytime routine gradually helps regulate nighttime sleep.
- Don't wait too late to put your baby to bed in the evening. Overtired babies resist sleep. Make changes gradually, though—it's ineffective to try to put your baby to bed two hours earlier all at once.
- Set up a bedtime routine that is repetitive and soothing. For example, a bath, then stories and singing in the rocking chair, then bed, at the same time every night.
- Get in the habit of using soothing words at bedtime. Pantley suggests, "ssshhhh" or a softly spoken phrase like "It's sleepy time." Some moms choose to sing the same song over and over while rocking. Soon your baby will associate those sounds with bedtime.
- Make your baby's room quiet and dark. White noise from an aquarium or a fan is often helpful. (At our house we have a fan on in the hallway for white noise at night.)
- Pantley suggested that even if you co-sleep, let your baby get used to his or her own bed as well. (Even when our babies were spending most of the night in our bed, I'd start them out in their own rooms, lying or sitting next to them to get them to sleep, then sneak off to

have another hour in the living room with my husband before we went to bed.)

- Make sure the sheets are cozy. (I will sometimes zap a tube sock full of rice in the microwave to use as a heating pad in the bed, removing it before laying the baby down.) Sleepwear should be soft and nonbinding. Tiny babies often sleep better when swaddled. But don't overdress your child or overheat the room.
- Don't respond to every noise your child makes. Learn to distinguish a real cry from a sleepy whimper. If you're not sure, it's okay to wait for a minute outside the door so you won't disturb him if he's actually asleep.

Remember, no single sleep strategy is effective with every baby—or even for one baby all the time. You'll have to get to know your child, be flexible, and figure out what works for you. Pantley wrote that when it comes to sleep training, parents have a choice between time and tears: "The irrefutable truth is that we cannot change a comfortable, loving-to-sleep (but waking-up-all-night) history to a go-to-sleep-and-stay-asleep-on-your-own routine without one of two things: crying or time. Personally, I choose time."[2]

A king-size bed is a great sanity-saver when you have little ones in your bed. Another option is a double mattress on the floor of your child's room, so that you have a comfortable place to rest when you go in to respond to your child at night. For years when my kids were little, I would go sit in their rooms with them while they fell asleep at night. I began this habit after Ben came home, when he and Josh wouldn't go to sleep unless I was in the room to remind them to be quiet and stay in bed.

I continued that tradition for our youngest daughters after they transitioned out of our bed into their own room. I probably could have skipped it for the girls—they were past toddler age. But they were still comforted by my presence, and by then in my mothering career, I understood that although some nights do seem to last forever, the years during which kids need their moms at night are very short. Soon enough they won't need you to get to sleep. Until then, why not meet their needs lovingly and enjoy your special position as the one who brings your child comfort at night?

Sleep and Older Children

When bringing home older children, night needs are often (though not always) less overwhelming. But many kids still do better sleeping with someone near them. Since our girls were nine and eleven on homecoming, and were used to sleeping together, we put them in a double bed together at first, sharing a room with their little sister, age five. A few weeks after they got home, they said they really would rather have their own beds. John obligingly built them bunk beds. But for months, we'd find them sleeping together in one single bunk in the morning. Obviously they needed the reassurance of each other more in the night than they realized.

One hard memory I have is of a time shortly after our older daughters arrived home. One evening our five-year-old was in a particularly hyper mood during bedtime stories. I told her she'd have to sleep with me instead of her dearly loved big sisters if she didn't settle down. My newly arrived nine-year-old daughter listened to that interchange and said, "I be bad, I sleep by your bed too?"

At the time, I was exhausted, and truthfully didn't expect even for our five-year-old to sleep with us. She adored sleeping with her big sisters. I imagined the certain lost sleep if *both* of them were flopping around on my bedroom floor and gently told my new daughter, no, she needed to sleep in her own bed with her big sister. I've thought of that moment many times since that day, and wish I'd been generous enough to give her a big hug and say, "Of course!"

As moms we often set certain ground rules to keep life flowing smoothly. Limits are important. But to be wise, we should always be willing to examine our "I could never do that" feelings to make sure they stand on valid ground. Too often our rules are based simply on convenience. And there are times when making an exception to a rule is not only appropriate but can be a powerful message of love to a struggling child.

One family let their new child sleep next to their bed for several weeks and then gradually moved the child's bed farther away from theirs, a few inches every night, until he finally ended up comfortably sleeping in his own room. Another friend of mine ended weeks of unhappy restlessness at night by allowing her two young daughters to sleep together. Only then did her newly arrived preschooler settle down and sleep well at night.

Feeding Newly Arrived Children

If you'd been watching me in the early weeks after our older daughters came home, you'd have seen me spending an awful lot of time cruising the grocery store aisles with a puzzled look on my face. During those first weeks, just about the only things they'd eat happily were rolls, peanut butter, rice, bananas, mangoes, and spaghetti sprinkled with berbere (an Ethiopian spice) and oil. I was constantly trying to find something to expand their repertoire.

One particularly memorable trip was all about jelly. Lidya said that Zeytuna liked jelly on her bread in Ethiopia, but hated the homemade raspberry jam that we typically ate. Maybe it was the seeds, I thought, and went on a jelly hunt. After several brands from Wal-Mart were rejected, I somehow ended up standing at Costco pondering a large box of single-pack servings of grape jelly—you know, the kind they serve in restaurants. I decided that if she ended up liking it, it'd be worth the cost, so home that jelly came, only to strike out as well.

Thankfully, the other kids thought it was great, so it wasn't a waste, but when I think back on those early days, I always remember that jelly. (These days, ironically, my girl hates store-bought jelly and jam, and only likes mine.)

When our kids first come home, we are primed to nurture them, and one of the ways we do so is with food. But food can be a minefield for families at first. The older the children are on homecoming, the more challenging food issues tend to be. Our two who came home as infants had fairly typical baby issues. Josh ended up being allergic to milk, but Julianna made the transition to American formula without a problem.

Our two toddlers were quite different from each other. Emily was a chubby thirty pounds on homecoming at twenty months. She happily gobbled almost anything we offered to her right from the start. Ben was about twenty-one pounds on homecoming and had many dislikes. His early struggles with attachment made it hard for him to accept food from me at times. He loved his bottles, but insisted on holding the bottle himself. That in itself is not so unusual for a kid his age, but he got upset if I even touched the bottle. He also couldn't tolerate eye contact while eating. He was okay with sitting on my lap for his bottle—his foster mom had obviously held him while bottle feeding—but he preferred to face outward in my arms.

It took lots of work to help him become more comfortable with cozy snuggles during bottle feeding. But gradually, as his attachment improved, his eating did too. For him there was a really strong connection between being comfortable with me and being able to accept food from me.

Our older girls came with a whole new level of food challenges. It makes sense—they'd had a decade eating a whole different type of diet. But it was a real blow to my ego as a cook—most people loved my cooking. Conscious of all the changes that had happened in their young lives, I made sure there were things they liked at each meal to fill in the cracks. But I also expected them to eat a few bites of everything I offered, a house rule that made them very unhappy for quite a while.

Julie Gumm (www.juliegumm.com), author of the book *Adopting Without Debt*, said, "Our kids were eight and nine when they came home, and food was our BIGGEST issue. For the first two weeks, people from church were bringing us meals, which was nice, but made it really difficult on the new kids who barely like anything. They ate a LOT of pasta, fruit, and peanut butter sandwiches those first few weeks. When I did start cooking, it didn't take me very long to realize it was best to keep things REALLY simple. No sauces, no gravy. Hamburgers, grilled chicken, etc. I made sure that their plate always had two things they liked and one new thing. Sometimes the new thing was the main course, sometimes it was a vegetable. We asked that they at least try one bite of the new food. If they didn't like it, they didn't have to eat more, and they could have as much of the other foods as they wanted. If the new thing was a main course, then they were welcome to make a peanut butter sandwich to replace it. One night we whipped out the Amharic phrasebook and went to the food section. It was then that we found out they liked white corn (HAD to be white) and sweet potatoes.

"We just kept with it. Sometimes there were things they weren't crazy about but would eat in small servings (like most vegetables). I just kept putting very small servings on their plate. We rewarded good attitudes and trying new foods with dessert, which was nothing more than those cheap frozen Otter Pops. Over time I was able to increase the serving size of those 'just okay' dishes, and inevitably over time they'd surprise me by going back for seconds.

"At least a year after they'd been home, we were eating dinner (chicken tetrazzini), and Luke exclaimed, 'What are these green things? They're really good. You should put more in next time.' They were green bell peppers. And he'd been picking them out of every dish for the last year."

Thankfully, Lidya had come to us already knowing how to cook a few things and showed me how to make several Ethiopian dishes that they enjoyed. In the early months we ate Ethiopian food at least a couple times a week. But I had a houseful of other people to please, so I continued to cook family favorites too.

As an experienced mom (ah, *that* stumbling block again!), I'd always believed that kids are picky because their parents allow it. For all our other kids, requiring a few bites each meal had eventually resulted in kids who would happily eat a huge variety of food.

But in the case of our daughters who spent a whole decade developing different tastes, it didn't work well at all. In fact, it turned meals from a chance to nurture into another battleground.

I knew I shouldn't take it personally, but at that point they were rejecting me on so many levels that every new slight felt personal. Everyone else loved my cooking. Everyone else thought I was a good mom. Everyone else loved me. But to them I was a failure on every level. Later, after our relationship improved, I found out that one of my girls had been a picky eater in Ethiopia too, and often turned down what her mother or grandmother offered her to eat. This tidbit comforted me; it was less about me than I'd assumed. But still each rejection stung.

Finally, after literally years of unhappy meals, I decided nurturing is more important than raising a "good" eater. These days if we're having mac and cheese, or if we're going out for much-hated tacos, I let kids make a peanut butter sandwich instead of suffering through food they hate. And as it turns out, food is deeply significant to the child who has the hardest time accepting nurture from me. She adores it when I set aside my idea of what constitutes a proper meal and feed her what she loves. And the funny thing is, the more often I choose to accommodate her tastes, the less aggravated I feel about it. I wish I'd released that control years ago. It truly helps her feel loved.

Angela Michelle wrote, "We adopted our daughter from foster care when she was two. Her palate was definitely adjusted to junk food, and she had come from a place where food was not provided with regularity. She didn't seem to really understand the concept of mealtime. She'd see food out on the counter as I made dinner and beg for it. It took her awhile to learn that we'd all eat together when the meal was ready. For the last seven years we've fed her breakfast, lunch, and dinner with consistency, but she remains anxious about food. As I pass out treats, she becomes visibly nervous, as if fearing she'll be missed. Now that she's older, to help her become aware of those lingering anxieties, I gently tease her and say, 'You know I'm about to give you a slice of this cake. You're going to really enjoy it.' There are many things I wish we had done differently, but one thing I'm grateful we did right was to avoid making food become an issue of tension or dispute with her. Since it's obviously an issue with deep emotional roots for her, we are careful not to add any baggage. As much as possible, we try not to comment on what or how she eats and emphasize that we will always provide as much as she needs."

The Bottomless Pit

Though many families experience picky eating in their newly arrived children, another common problem families have is a child who doesn't seem to know when to stop eating. Some kids even become clinically obese in those first months or years home.

This happens most often with kids who experienced food deprivation in infancy and early childhood. It's something that can be really hard to handle. Food is so intimately tied with nurturing that it can be very difficult to refuse a child food, even if he's obviously had too much. Some kids will get very distressed if food is withheld and then literally eat until they vomit.

Other children will get up at night to steal food and eat it secretly in bed. This can be hugely frustrating to parents, who feel like kids are flouting limits and being disobedient. Sometimes parents will lock up all food or put alarms on the child's door so that they'll know when the child is getting up. But this does little to solve the underlying problem: this child doesn't believe food will always be available and feels desperate to take control of the problem. Even kids who've been home for years can still feel insecure about food. Susan Emmett, an adoption specialist and social worker, said it is crucial to give kids control: "These kids, even adopted as toddlers, must have full control over the food. It also is essential in bonding. Withhold food for any reason, and you set the bonding cycle back months."[3]

Some parents pack snacks into a fanny pack for their anxious child to eat whenever she feels hungry, or set a basket of snacks on the dining room table, healthy food that's accessible anytime. If night eating is an issue, it might work to set a basket of snacks next to the child's bed so that she will know there's something to eat whenever she needs it. Ultimately, the parents who successfully navigated the choppy waters of food issues say that the most important thing is to keep trying, keep reassuring, and as much as possible stay relaxed so that mealtime can eventually be a time of joy and nurturing.

> Marissa wrote, "Just a couple weeks ago my two oldest Ethiopian kiddos started eating salad. Yes, salad. This was worthy of celebration as the past three years in our home have been salad free . . . and I love salad. I've been really impressed with how far they've come when it comes to food. I'll never forget my son hiding chewed-up green

beans in his cheeks at the dinner table so he could spit it
in the toilet.

"In my experience, it's all about patience and main-
taining a sense of joy around mealtime. Every meal had to
include a healthy protein, a veggie, and a whole grain, but if
they didn't like what I was serving they could opt for something else that fit the criteria. In the end, our kids have told me
they wanted to like the foods I served because food is such
a celebration in our family. It's more fun to fully participate."

Nurturing Your Marriage

After a new child comes home, it can be tricky to figure out how
to nurture both the new relationship with your child and the existing relationship with your partner. People these days tend to think
that going out on dates with your spouse is an essential part of a
healthy relationship. New moms sometimes feel pressured to have
time away from their newly arrived babies and toddlers, even if
their guts are screaming that the child isn't ready. Especially with
newly adopted children, it is crucial to remember the foundational
importance of attachment.

I think that we moms subconsciously notice a whole array of
things about our children that we may not even be able to verbalize,
but that help us form our opinions about their abilities and needs.
I personally have found that when my kids are ready to be away
from me, my anxiety about leaving them diminishes. Our younger-
adopted kids all came home between four and twenty months, and
it took me a year or *more* each time before I left them with anyone
but John, and then only for a short time.

So what about dates? Certainly some children are comfortable enough fairly soon after homecoming that mom and dad could go out for an hour or two without harm. If you can pull off a date now and then without causing terror and regression to your baby, then go for it. But if a couple hours away causes your newly arrived child to regress and act insecure for days afterward, consider nurturing your relationship with your partner in other ways for a while.

Home "Dates"

Chat late at night. Plan a special candlelit dinner on the patio after your child is in bed. Talk in the morning over coffee while your child watches *Curious George*. Take time to text message each other during the day. Kiss long and passionately on homecoming despite the one-year-old standing on the floor between your knees. John and I especially like to kiss in front of our teens; it's fun to hear them groan.

Dates aren't what is important; connection is. It is possible to nurture the connection between mom and dad *and* the connection to your newly arrived child. In time, dating can make a comeback. But if you don't yet feel peace about leaving your newly arrived little one, don't feel guilty about waiting until your child is ready.

Though John and I didn't do a lot of dating while all our children were small, when our older girls came home and life felt very challenging, we quickly decided that a couple dates a month were good for everyone. The kids got fish sticks and a movie with their older siblings, and John and I got to have some uninterrupted conversation.

Typically an evening would begin as a rehash of that week's challenges, then move into discussing ways to parent with wisdom. Parenting was harder on me than on John, since I was there all the time. Until we really started talking about what was happening, he didn't quite understand why I was so frazzled. He didn't need a blow-by-blow report of *everything* that happened, but he needed to hear the overall story to be able support me with wisdom.

Though much of the talk was about our kids, unfailingly we'd head back home with more energy and perspective with which to begin the new week. Because we pulled together during those hard times, our marriage relationship became stronger, something I count as a great blessing during that hard time.

Therefore, as God's chosen people, holy and dearly loved, clothe yourselves with compassion, kindness, humility, gentleness and patience. Bear with each other and forgive one another if any of you has a grievance against someone. Forgive as the Lord forgave you. And over all these virtues put on love, which binds them all together in perfect unity.

COLOSSIANS 3:12–14

CHAPTER 7

When You're Down to
Your Last Drop of Faith

MANY MOMMAS GO INTO ADOPTION WITH THE IDEA that after a year or two of newness, kids will settle in and life will get back to normal. A new normal, surely, but something that feels comfortable and livable. I was one of those mommas, and with our younger-adopted children, that's pretty much how it went. Connection sprang up within days with three of our babies, at least in my heart, with the fourth needing about a year to feel well settled. But when preparing for the arrival of our older girls, oh, my expectations were naive.

As I wrote this book, several news stories featured adoptions that had gone wrong. Some stories involved horrific, inexcusable abuse. My heart breaks for those children; what was done to them is wrong, wrong, wrong. No behavior of theirs, however difficult, deserved that response. But I also mourn the lost dreams of the parents, who most likely began with good intent, but had no idea how inadequate their own emotional resources were to parent wounded souls.

Then there are the families who struggle for years to parent wisely and well, but end up having to disrupt an adoption and relinquish a child to be raised by others. Folks who haven't parented a difficult child often judge parents who disrupt very harshly. But very often in cases like this, children have become abusive toward others in their families to a degree that makes parents realize they are no longer able to keep everyone safe.

It's a nightmare of misery for everyone involved. Every adoptive mom wants to end up being her child's forever mom, and it's heartbreaking to realize sometimes it is necessary to mother a child from a distance—to set aside her own dreams, to pray and hope for the child's future, but to leave the daily nurturing to someone else. Sometimes, in situations where no bonding has happened and parents have exhausted every resource, a brand-new start is exactly what the child needs. I know of several such disruptions where children were moved to new families (usually where they were placed as the youngest child instead of somewhere in the middle) and with good counseling and support went on to thrive and do well. Other children can benefit from temporary placement in residential care, where after a time of intensive, focused therapy, they eventually are able to live in their families again.

John and I have never considered disrupting the adoption of any of our children. But we also have blessedly never endured the far extremes of difficult behavior. We haven't ever feared for our own lives or for the safety of our children. But I have nothing but respect and sympathy for families who've walked hard paths, exhausted every resource, and finally made the heartbreaking decision that they needed to be a child's in-between family, not his or her forever family. These families need the love and support of everyone around them.

However, even parenting kids somewhere in the middle of the "difficulty" spectrum can drain a parent's emotional energy and resources in ways that are impossible to understand unless you've lived it. During our girls' early weeks at home, it was relatively easy to be patient. Everything was new, and they had so many reasons to be grieving. No wonder things were hard.

Six months passed, and I wondered why things were still so very hard. Twelve months in, improvement was miniscule. Two years in, and we were battle weary, but the battle was still going strong. Three and four years in, we were beginning to see some growth, praise God. But there were still many days that felt exactly like that hard first year. When our children's grieving didn't follow our expected time line, and problem behaviors did not go away, patience became harder and harder to find.

And here's the thing: it's easy to imagine being patient with a child whom you only know as a picture on your fridge with a sad life story. But when you get up every morning with the best intentions, determined to work for growth in the relationship, and are rejected day after day after day, pain can begin to overshadow the compassion you felt so easily in the beginning.

Of course all kids sass and push parents away sometimes. What's different about parenting a hurt child is the sheer number of distancing behaviors. Whether or not they realize it, attachment-challenged kids are terrified of connection. This fear leads them to avoid or sabotage moments of connection over and over again, sometimes dozens of times in an hour. By the end of the day, even the most well-intentioned, educated momma feels battle fatigue—because in the midst of all that opposition, we're there reaching out and nurturing and loving anyway. Loving a resistant kid is a hugely draining proposition. In fact, post-traumatic stress disorder is a very real diagnosis for many folks parenting kids with attachment issues. Moms of well-attached kids have difficulty during the tumultuous teen years too. But they have something to sustain them that moms of older-adopted kids don't have: memories of good moments together. Moments of rocking babies to sleep when they were tiny, laughing with them, reaching down to pick them up when they stretched their arms out to you. Those lovely back-and-forth moments of giving and receiving nurture remain in a mom's memory bank and make hard moments during the teen years easier to bear.

I came to understand the love of Jesus on a much deeper level during those oh-so-hard early years. I came to be in awe at the kind of love that tirelessly yet gently pursues a heart when being rejected, that shows grace in the face of hateful words, that chooses to hope even when relationship sometimes can feel like a hopeless dream. As parents we truly can only love in this way when we're being empowered by Jesus moment by moment.

It also helps to remind ourselves of the deep hurt our children have experienced. Some older-adopted children have never gotten good nurturing. They don't know how to be in a relationship. Others have wonderful memories of being loved and cared for by their first moms. That love is a huge blessing, but it also divides kids' loyalties, and it can make it hard to accept love from a new mom. The very act of nurture stirs up sadness in the child and reminds him of his loss.

Parents aren't the only ones who get worn down by negative interaction. Kids often come into adoption with idealistic imaginings too. Many expect life in America to be full of material possessions, with parents who cater to their every whim. My girls got parents who assign chores and expect them to learn their multiplication tables and are sometimes hardnosed when kids balk and sass.

Rarely do parents completely understand how much pain the child is feeling; I know we didn't. Past hurt doesn't evaporate when a child comes into a loving family; it marches into the home right along with the child, distorting a child's beliefs about his own goodness and worth, and making it hard for him to accept our love and trust our good intent.

A War Zone

By the time our girls had been home a few months, our home began to feel like a war zone. Fiery darts of anger and defiance flew everywhere, even at simple requests. Nothing was easy. For the sake of the little sisters watching and beginning to imitate them, we knew we couldn't overlook difficult behaviors. We still remembered the pain the girls had experienced, but we mourned the changed atmosphere of our home. We wanted to find a way to respect their loss while also honoring the limits and rules we'd always valued in our home. That turned out to be a much taller order than we realized.

But we plunged in gamely anyway, using tools that had worked well with our other children in the past. We put a chart on the side of the fridge that spelled out our expectations and tied them to privileges, things like TV time and outings and youth group, and to consequences, things like early bedtimes and weeding flowerbeds and missing outings that they enjoyed. I had high hopes that with clearly defined rules and predictable consistency, things might get better.

Well, the kids who were well bonded to us slipped and lost privileges now and then, but they made good choices most of the time. The kids we most wanted to influence balked at the chart, and would over and over sabotage their chances to get good things—in a way that almost seemed deliberate at times. Some seemed to prefer being at the bottom of the chart, with no privileges left to lose.

We tried different rewards, different consequences, thinking if we could find the right motivators, things would turn around. Each new consequence became another thing they chose not to care about. Early bedtime backfired for kids who were skeevy about family time anyway. They preferred bed over stories with Dad. Floor scrubbing was easier than doing schoolwork. Time-out in the bedroom or time weeding flowerbeds was better than sitting in the living room homeschooling with Mom. Facebook? Don't need it. Youth group? Who cares.

We were grasping at oil, trying to find something they cared about. But that was exactly the problem. Their hearts were so full of hurt that they didn't *want* to care, especially about John and me. It was more comfortable to keep us at arm's length, to see us as privilege stealers, as enemies.

I longed for success, prayed for it fervently, and hated taking away privileges. I'd give extra chances, then feel crushed when they still chose disobedience and I had to follow through with consequences anyway. Then I'd worry that giving grace was undermining my authority or that consequences were alienating them more.

I got wise counsel. I read book after book after book. I hugged them and talked to them and cried over them and prayed for them and apologized when I lost my patience. (Because, boy, I did, sometimes.) Always, I longed to touch their hearts. I woke every morning and came out with a smile to greet them for the day, and over and over again was greeted with sour rejection.

Now and then, usually when they were interacting with other people, I caught glimpses of the beautiful souls buried under all the anger. It was those souls I was pursuing, that I couldn't bear to stop pursuing. But their pain caused them to see me as *the* major problem in their lives, and not a solution to anything.

The continual rejection was wearing me down, gradually ripping bigger and bigger chunks out of my heart. I'd never felt so hated in my life. I began to feel mixed up and myopic, with tender spots from being jabbed over and over every day, in hundreds of little ways.

I was beginning to suffer from serious compassion fatigue. I didn't doubt our decision to adopt—God had led us incredibly clearly down this path. But oh, I longed for some positive feedback—a hug or a smile now and then. I wanted the girls to understand how much I wanted good for them. I dreamed of the day they'd tell me what was going on in their hearts. I longed for them to feel like true daughters—or even the beginning glimmers of a relationship headed that direction. Instead, it felt like we were housing surly boarders.

Understanding Minds and Hearts

Looking objectively at our daughters' behaviors compared to other adopted kids, all along I knew they were somewhere in the middle of the spectrum. There was tons of rudeness and anger, lots of resistance to affection. It was not easy. But they were almost unfailingly appropriate out in public. They weren't threatening us physically. They were often kind to their younger siblings and were incredibly sweet with babies. Oh, I had hope when I saw how they played with babies. It was then that I could clearly see the sweetness at the core of their hearts. I've always felt like my best, truest self when I'm around babies. That seemed true for my girls too. And those baby lovers—we could get along with each other, I was sure. So why weren't things working for us? What wasn't I understanding?

Hijacking the Thinking Brain

Back to the books I went, reading more about brain development and the effects of trauma on children. I've already mentioned the book *The Whole-Brain Child*, where Dr. Daniel Siegel talked about the upstairs brain and the downstairs brain. Remember, the upstairs brain is responsible for logical thought and problem solving, and the downstairs brain is the instinctive brain, the one that causes you to blink when something flies at your face, or startle when someone jumps out and scares you. Kids who've experienced trauma have overactive downstairs brains, which causes them to descend into fight-or-flight thinking very quickly. Almost anything can trigger that downstairs brain: hunger; dark bedrooms; scratchy clothing; loud, chaotic environments; and a host of other things. Kids don't even have to be old enough to remember the event to be triggered by something similar.

Several months ago I brought our toddler grandson, Ranger, into our chicken house to gather eggs. Just as we walked into the dim space, the rooster, perched next to our heads, crowed loudly. Ranger saw and heard the rooster all in the same instant and burst into terrified screaming. Months later I once again brought Ranger into the chicken house to gather eggs, not realizing he'd even remember his past fear. But the moment the door creaked open and he saw into the dim space, his whole body stiffened. Frantic, he wrapped his arms and legs around me with every ounce of his strength and burst into tears. Obviously he remembered his past terror, even though no physical hurt had ever happened to him in that chicken house.

Once a child descends into that fight-or-flight mode, her upstairs brain becomes temporarily unavailable, making logical thinking almost impossible. And yet so many times I've tried to talk logic to an upset kid. Upset adults too, for that matter. No wonder I didn't feel like I was getting anywhere. The thinking brain had checked out. Only when a person regains her calm can she return to her thinking brain and hear what you have to say.

Riding the River

Another thing that can happen during stress is a disconnect from the right brain, the side of the brain that has direct access to bodily sensations and emotional states. Stressed kids often feel more comfortable living in the left (analytical) brain, disconnected from all those scary emotions.

People who've coped with stress by shutting down their right brains won't be able to talk about their emotions, said Dr. Siegel. "If someone asks them how they feel or what's going on in their bodies, they will say 'I don't know what you're talking about.' They live in the 'Land of the Left,' and if you try to go right-hemisphere to right-hemisphere with them too soon, they become emotionally flooded."[1]

In *The Whole-Brain Child*, Siegel described the balance between emotion and logic as a "river of well-being," with chaos (emotion) on the right bank and control (logic) on the left bank. When we are feeling emotionally balanced, we are in the middle of the river, able to navigate small bumps with a calm and relaxed attitude, using the strengths from both the logical and emotional sides of our brains. When we get off-balance and distressed, we tend to go in one of two directions, either to the right bank of that river, where emotions can drag us helter-skelter, or to the left bank, where we ignore emotion and try to exert control over a difficult situation to end the stress.[2]

Everyone has tendencies in one direction or the other. I tend to handle stress by going left-brain and trying to control and logic my kids back to a more stable place emotionally. Problem is, kids who are in their right brain often can't hear logic. Instead, they'll be focused on things like facial expression, tone of voice, and the intensity level with which I'm speaking. If I'm speaking angrily, even if I'm honestly trying to help, they'll register my anger, not my words. I've got to reach out, right brain to right brain, and find a way to lovingly validate their emotions.

Address Emotions First

Not long ago during an interaction with one of my more right-brain kids, I realized we were heading for that familiar logjam again—with her flooded with emotion and me trying to use logic to settle her down. I apologized and reached out for a hug, saying sincerely, "Oh, this is really hard! I'm so sorry."

Sometimes she resists my hugs, but this time she heard the honest unhappiness in my voice and melted into my embrace. We went on to have a good conversation. I think that moment went well because I remembered to first acknowledge her feelings, and reached out to touch her in a warm and caring way. That validated her feelings enough that she was then able to listen to my logic.

Kids who mostly live in left-brain land, on the other hand, often are out of touch with their feelings. Sometimes physical sensations don't even register. A child can have goose bumps all over her arms, with skin that is cold to the touch, and deny that she feels cold. Emotions can be equally mysterious to these types of kids—they're often more comfortable believing they don't have emotions. Or the only emotion they'll admit to is anger. That's the least scary and feels the most powerful. And almost categorically they'll blame that anger on others.

Lately I've been working on talking with all my kids about their feelings, especially those who are less emotionally aware. One thing we've talked about is that anger is a cover-up emotion; there are always more vulnerable feelings underneath. I may not be able to coach them to be fully self-aware; I'm still working on it myself. But I see huge potential in being willing to go there with our kids, even if it gets ugly at times, even if their feelings are hard to face.

Faith

I believe faith is intimately involved in the balancing act between the right and left brain. Often when we get out of balance, veering right toward emotional chaos or left toward a white-knuckle attempt at controlling our lives, it's because we've taken our eyes off Jesus and are looking instead to people or circumstances for emotional satisfaction. Remembering that our hope is in the Lord makes it easier to stay in the middle of that emotional river, aware of emotions but not letting them take over, able to use logic without clawing desperately for control.

Another thing that sends me veering toward one bank or another of that river is when, temporarily at least, I buy in to various lies about parenting. Sometimes it's the lie that my child's behavior reflects on me as a parent. That's not true. We all have a sin nature, and my child's behavior, right or wrong, in the long run is between him and God.

Another lie that can shanghai me is the belief that if I don't deal with this behavior (correctly) right now, my child will struggle with this issue forever. Hopelessness can grip me and leave me feeling like nothing I do will make a difference. That discounts the truth that God *is* at work in my child's life right now. Because of Jesus, we always have hope. He is never giving up on us, nor will He give up on our kids. Are there lies that steal your peace? How can you counter those lies with truth?

Adoption and Abandonment

Many times with an adopted child, there are issues of abandonment. Most adults understand that relinquishment is about difficult circumstances in the parents' lives, and not about the child at all. But kids often don't understand that until they're grown themselves, and even then adoptees sometimes have tiny aching doubts about why their first families chose not to parent. Whatever the reason, it was a point in their lives when it felt like a loved one didn't love them well enough to stick around and care for them. Some adoptees spend the rest of their lives on high alert for more confirmation that others also find them not good enough. Sometimes adoptive parents play right into that fear without even realizing it.

Michelle said, "It took me years to figure out the origin of one of my daughter's biggest triggers. She was hypervigilant about fairness, and always seemed to be looking for ways that Jeff and I might be treating her less well than our biological children. Sometimes we did have to parent her differently. We avoided scary movies with her for years because we felt like her past had been scary enough. And due to her maturity level, we waited to give her some freedoms that we allowed older siblings to have sooner. But it took me a long time to realize that her hypervigilance was not only about us and those perceived injustices. It was about her past, a past where a member of her extended family had relinquished her, while still choosing to parent their own children. It happened once—how could she not wonder if it might happen again?"

My Emotions Matter Too

As I read about brain integration and trauma and brain maturation, I began to have just as many lightbulb moments about myself as I did about the girls. For the first time I saw how my issues might be impacting my hurting daughters. Well-bonded kids are resilient and secure enough to thrive with a wide range of parenting styles. Kids from hard places don't have the secure emotional base that helps them weather parental ups and downs.

I've always thought of myself as competent and capable, even wise at times. But the truth is, I've got my share of sore spots. When my well-bonded kids inadvertently bumped into those sore spots of mine, my unhappy reaction and their love for me caused them to back off and avoid that spot the next time. They knew I loved them even when I was grumpy. My hurting kids didn't have any of that natural concern, nor did they fully believe I loved them. They were constantly poking, constantly testing every single sore spot, every weakness, every fear, even ones I never realized I had.

I'm not unusual. Nobody gets a perfect childhood. The childhood moments that left us feeling vulnerable and powerless can reach out and grab us in all sorts of unexpected ways in adulthood, especially when we're under stress. And believe me, there's not much in life more stressful than parenting a child who is actively rejecting and defying you.

Dr. Laura Markham, who writes a blog at www.ahaparenting .com, said that whenever we are triggered, most likely we've stumbled on something that needs healing in our psyches. "Any time your child pushes your buttons, you can bet those buttons were installed in your own childhood."[3]

Tricia (www.inpursuitofatoolbox.com) said, "To be a 'successful' adoptive mom, I have had to look honestly and deeply at what I bring to the table and work very hard to change the dynamics so that we can all be as healthy as possible. This has happened through reading, changing my parenting paradigm, therapy, and through brokenness. This has been quite a journey about changing me and forming me into who God desires."

In my case, I had a rather volatile dad, one whose own emotional reactions took up so much space in the family that there wasn't room for anyone else's feelings. I never doubted his love for us—he loved just as passionately as he expressed his frustrations. But he was not an easy person to live with.

My mom is a nurturing peacemaker. She loved us and my dad well, smoothing out the bumps in his life as best as she could, and she continues to love us all well. But because of my dad (who died when I was twenty), I grew up without much voice and had almost no practice at constructive conflict resolution. One of my core childhood messages was that disagreement is bad.

Most of the time I did fairly well at parenting my kids who'd been with me since babyhood. When our older-adopted kids introduced a new level of conflict into our home, it sent me straight into my fight-or-flight brain. Forget parenting that nurtures. I desperately needed the conflict done.

For years I sensed that the level of frustration I was feeling at times was not quite logical. My kids weren't waving knives at me. And no parent ever died from being sassed. But the sassier my kids were, the less able I was to parent thoughtfully. Plain and simple, I was being triggered. Over and over. It was rare to get through a day without a major disrespect. The more often it happened, the more I clamped down in hopes of making it end. Except instead of ending the sass, it just triggered more anger and fear in them and made them more likely to sass. In the early months and years after a child comes home, it is very normal for improvement to be slow. Three steps forward and two steps backward is pretty common. But overall it should feel like there's a trend in the right direction. I wanted to think we were heading in the right direction after our older girls came home, but looking back honestly, I think for a while I was so intent on making change happen that I was alienating the girls and adding to their unhappiness.

What I Needed to Give Up:
Anger over Disrespect

As I trudged through that valley, one of the best things I did for myself and for my kids was to figure out which scenarios were most often triggering my frustration. A big one for me is disrespect. When I was growing up, I'd never have dared to talk to my parents the way some of my kids speak to me in times of frustration. When I hear certain attitudes coming at me from my kids, I'm flooded with indignation. They're sinning against me, and it's wrong.

But—this point is *huge* to remember with hurting children—kids inflict pain because of pain they've experienced. A knee scarred from surgery often will lose some normal range of motion. In the same way, the scars on my child's heart impinge on his heart's ability to respond normally. Hurt people tend to hurt other people.

And—this was just as important for me to realize—the reaction that comes from me when I am muttering about their wrongness is just as sinful, just as unloving as what my kids are doing to me.

Our thoughts can either calm and soothe us, leading us toward right action, or they can fuel our frustration and cause us to sin against those we love. Sure, we can tell ourselves our anger is righteous. You know, "Be angry and sin not." Jesus was angry when He threw the money changers out of the temple. But we're not Jesus. Most likely if we're mad enough to spit, we're sinning, plain and simple. We've got to approach this job with humility, remembering just how much we ourselves have sinned against our Savior. When we get haughty and forgetful, Satan can get us reacting sinfully in a heartbeat. Do you think healing happens there? Not in a million years.

What I Needed to Give Up: My "Ideal" Mother-Child Relationship

Another thing I had to give to God was my longing for an "ideal" momma-child relationship. That was one of the longings that led me to adopt in the first place. And, oh, I've been blessed with so much sweet time with each and *every one* of my precious ones. I would have missed so many blessings if we had not chosen to adopt. I am eternally grateful to God for tugging our hearts along this journey.

But there's also been much pain and rejection. I expected it early on, but years down the road, when you've invested years of love and prayer, it can be incredibly hard to hear a kid say, "I hate you. You'll never be my mom." Even when you know those words were hasty and spoken in anger, they cut deep.

Attachment challenges steal the very moments that you most long for as a mother. I cling to the hope that more of those moments will happen as our kids move toward maturity. And in fact, as I become better at loving steadily and openhandedly, without expecting them to love me back, I already see it happening in wonderful ways, praise God.

But our relationship may always be more complicated than if we'd been able to share precious moments when they were tiny. In fact, one mom suggested it might be more realistic to see yourself playing the role of wise aunt to an older-adopted child rather than longing for and possibly never getting the place of mother in their hearts. Does that thought make your heart hurt? It does mine. I want to be the momma, not an aunty to my girls. Oh, it's painful to give up dreams. But the more lightly I hold on to my own dreams and desires, the better I can love my girls.

One of my kids hates hugs. For years I hugged anyway, and I still do, sometimes. That's what mommas do. But I finally realized that child actually sees hugs as control and harassment and not at all the act of love that I intend it. I don't think it is healthy for a child not to be hugged at all. But as an act of love toward this particular child, I'm choosing to hug less often and more briefly. But there's much pain in that offering. Sometimes I feel like a child myself, sitting amid broken dreams, longing for more relationship than my children are able to give right now.

But even in the hardest moments, I'm comforted to know that it is God who led us on this path. He doesn't make mistakes. I'm not offering up my dreams to my children. I'm offering them up to my Savior who knows my heart and sees my soul and who sacrificed everything for me. And He is Jehovah Rapha, the Healer.

There may still be great joy, great victory for us later on. But if that's not the reality today, I'm better off embracing what *is*, and reminding myself that God in His infinite mercy put me with my precious ones just as we are—fallible, wounded humans who sometimes struggle greatly to love one another. I choose to trust His wisdom, and I choose to love God by loving this child, whether improvement is quick or slow or almost invisible. Or perhaps not even until heaven.

Kristen said, "I think for my son, whom we adopted from Ethiopia when he was almost five, the biggest challenge and surprise was that love and time (so far) doesn't heal all wounds. He was abandoned by an aunt who said she would come back for him and didn't, and his mother passed away while he was in the orphanage. His inability to trust and his anger with his biological mother and aunt colors his relationship with me every. single. day. It also deeply affects my relationship with my husband because my adopted son only allows his father to truly parent him, which can make me resentful. Of course I want a deep relationship with my son. I've had to mourn the loss of what I thought that relationship would be for now and accept it for what it is. I have none of these issues with our youngest son, who was adopted from Ethiopia when he was six months old. When I can make my son laugh is when I feel the most connected to him. It seems like when I can crack a joke or point out something silly, he allows me into his world, and his trust issues melt away for just a moment."

What I Needed to Give Up: My Old "Rules and Consequences" Parenting Style

Wow, this was a hard one, and something that we are still laying down over and over, day by day. John and I were really successful parents with our big kids. Frankly, that's one of the reasons we were brave enough to attempt older-child adoption. But we didn't understand how differently we'd need to parent to be successful with a child from hard places.

Jennifer Anderson, a licensed marriage and family therapist, said, "Many moms parented neuro-typical bio children before their adoptive children and did a beautiful job. Most [of them were] very good moms with earlier children . . . but then had to find a NEW way to successfully parent children from a hard place. More sweat, tears, crying, screaming, introspection, soul searching, compromise, reevaluating, wishing, praying, and begging at times for a new perspective that will meet the needs of the child that is struggling in the here and now."

John and I assumed that once their behavior improved, our relationship would grow too. We didn't realize for years that we had that little equation exactly backward. It goes: first relationship, then behavior. It's how we did it with our babies, right? We build the relationship for many months, saying yes to their needs thousands of times before we ever add in behavior expectations. But somehow with our hurt kids, we expect all sorts of things just because they're older. Well, guess what? Relationship still needs to come first. The more we tried to change our kids' behavior via consequences before we had the relationship piece in place, the further their hurt hearts fled. The more I tried to encourage right behavior using typical parenting methods, the more like a drill sergeant I became. The gentle, patient, intuitive part of my soul was getting buried. And drill sergeants aren't so easy to bond with. I had to take control of my frustration and learn a new way to relate, one that looked a lot more like the love that comes from Jesus. Instead of being a nagging taskmaster, I needed to be a channel of His grace.

Sometimes we'd have lovely moments, usually when I pretended not to see rudeness and remembered the power of humor. We'd feel connected for a little while, and my hope would flare high. Maybe finally all our hard work was paying off. But each small success, so encouraging to me, seemed to bring out fear full force in the child. The next day would be awful, with me waking optimistically, only to discover that the nice moments of the previous day had put the child in full relationship retreat, intent on pushing *all* my buttons. Must. Make. Mom. Go. Away.

It made me think of the arcade game where you get a hammer and try to whack moles as they pop out of holes. That was my life, with mole after mole popping up over and over and me whacking away grimly. What I didn't think about for quite a while is that those moles are powered by invisible mechanisms under the surface. It was the same with our daughters' behaviors.

Nikki brought home her son Lemuel at age eight, after he'd spent most of his life in orphanages and endured multiple failed placements in the United States: "We thought it would be easy. We were critical of all who had gone before us. Until we were humbled. Until we couldn't fix him either. We came to the stark realization that when handed a body bag with a broken person inside, we expected him to 'rise up and walk' just by virtue of living under our blessed roof. We somehow fancied our mere presence sufficient to heal this child.

"Fast-forward five years. Lemuel is still in our family. He has been in counseling and residential treatment since joining our crew. We have made many mistakes in our parenting of him. We have held the bar so high that he could never jump over it and then been furious when he didn't. We have failed. But we have also succeeded. We promised him that this family would be his last stop. And it is. Not because we are so tolerant or so perfect and certainly not because he has been 'cured' of all his issues.

"This is Lemuel's last stop because he is our child and we love him. We are learning to accept him 'as is.' We don't have the kind of glue that mends a broken child, but we have a heavenly Father who makes all things new, and He is teaching us bit by bit and day by day that He is sovereign. Lemuel has improved GREATLY over the last five years but, guess what? So have we. We have learned the meaning of 'blessing in disguise,' and we are working on figuring out other mysteries like 'unconditional love' and 'adjusting expectations.'"

I didn't understand that for kids who aren't yet bonded, even simple expectations are like asking Lazarus to come forth from the grave. Instead of whacking the moles of rudeness and disrespect, I was going to need to go deeper, to address the pain, and to pursue relationship above all else. Kids don't want to please you until they care about you.

In the midst of the struggle, God kept bringing Romans 2:4 to my mind: "God's kindness is intended to lead you to repentance." Love is most winsome when we realize how wholly undeserved it is. But there I was, saying to the girls, "Be better, do better, and then all our problems will be solved." Not so loving, and not remotely grace-filled.

It was actually the arrival of our first grandbabies that reminded me who I really am. I found myself using the intuitive, gentle bits of myself, and thinking of how rusty that felt. I am my best, truest self when I'm around babies. I can read their body language. I can coax and soothe and anticipate needs. As I played with those precious babies, I often felt my girls' eyes drawn to my face, watching me. Inside I was crying out, "See, this is the real me. This is the me that has been getting lost during this terrible battle. I want to love you like this too, if only you would stop pushing me away."

The girls' pushing-away behaviors were so constant that it felt as though nearly every interaction required correction. But for their hearts to be won by me, they needed to see the intuitive, gentle momma that I was with those babies, not the stern and wounded warrior that I had become.

I needed to set aside my hurt, to major in the majors, and to love them without looking for anything in return. I needed to figure out how to say yes way more often, say no way less often and with much more love. I needed to show my precious ones *His* kind of love, love brave enough to enter the lions' den, willing to endure pain in the pursuit of their hearts. Jesus' love is way better than Mary's love. I knew it. But how could I live it?

> Jennifer said, "Once I let go of consequences and behaviors and truly started focusing all my energy on feelings, things have gotten much better for all of us. Those are the moments when I feel very successful and connected with my son—when he and I both know something unlovable happened yet my love remains, unwavering. I can almost feel the relief oozing from his pores in those moments."

Helping Our Children Be Stable

To best help our children, we first need to thoughtfully assess the times that we ourselves descend into dysregulation and think through why those situations challenge us. And here's a hint: if the first answer that pops into your mind is, "It's because my child . . . ," you probably need to think a little deeper about your own junk. Sure, our kids have issues. But their issues don't *cause* our issues; they only *uncover* them. We all have childhood wounds, some small and some larger.

Daniel Siegel found that one trait of high functioning adults is the ability to make sense of their stories, even the hard parts: "Without a coherent narrative that gives us a foundation for understanding ourselves and how the past has impacted who we are, we are often quite challenged to be fully present as a parent and remain receptive to who our child is."[4]

To help a child really heal and grow in times of emotional stress, we parents need to enter into our child's emotional experience without losing our emotional stability. If our own frustration runs away with our common sense in the midst of an interaction, we can't offer our kids calming attunement. When we're angry, we won't be able to help our kids out of a paper bag, let alone navigate them past their own incredibly painful emotional turmoil.

Hurt kids desperately need *high* functioning parents. Only by getting a handle on our own triggers and frustrations can we stay calm, then help our children feel understood and find their own ways to calm. It's a delicate dance. In the case of a child who has a chaotic attachment style, we may not be able to connect perfectly. But over time, managing our own triggers makes it much more likely that we can help our children learn self-regulation too.

The really great thing is that just naming a trigger will almost immediately give it a little less power over you. It's oddly calming to be able to tell yourself, *Oh yes, that's one of my triggers. Take a deep breath. It's okay.*

The more often we catch ourselves blaming our kids for relationship issues, the more likely it is that we also have work of our own to do. It takes honesty and courage and a great big dose of humility to dig around and figure out why we're struggling to respond lovingly in hard moments. Some parents may be able to travel this journey on their own, but I suspect that many of us would benefit from counseling to get there more quickly. I had no idea when I began this adoption journey that God had as much growth planned for supposedly grown-up me as He did my children.

Parenting a child who is afraid to attach is tremendously challenging work. If you have the chance to support a momma in the midst of this heroic struggle, do it prayerfully, wholeheartedly, and without judgment. Often challenging children look normal out in the world. People on the outside wonder if the mother is overreacting, hypercritical, or not trying hard enough. Instead of judging, lift her up in prayer. Support her sympathetically in every way that you can. The battle is epic. The stakes are beyond any price: we are battling for the hearts of our children.

Jennifer Anderson, LMFT, is an adoptive mother and a therapist who practices in Lone Tree, Colorado. "I think it's very challenging for many to take full responsibility for their triggers and avoid falling into the [trap of assuming] 'I just have a hard kid . . .' or 'If he/she would___, then I could attach and be calm.' It's much easier to blame the child. Parents have to do their part too. . . . I had my own wake-up moment one day when I realized that I couldn't do the same things I was doing anymore. I needed to show up in a new way for my kids, even though it was hard, scary, and exhausting. Shortly after that moment, things started to shift a lot in the attachment dance. I realize that for some parents, even after all of their hard introspective work, giving felt safety and voice, empowering the child to succeed, and connecting to their heart, depending on the level of the kid's trauma, [the child] still may not fully be able to mold into connection with the parent. But at least moms can rest knowing they have brought everything to the table that they could, that they showed up in the most authentic, connecting, and attuned way possible."

This is how we know what love is: Jesus Christ laid down his life for us. And we ought to lay down our lives for our brothers and sisters. . . . Dear children, let us not love with words or speech but with actions and in truth.

1 JOHN 3:16, 18

Beginning Again, at the Foot of the Cross

YOU MAY HAVE HEARD THE OLD SAYING THAT THE definition of insanity is doing the same thing over and over and expecting different results. In the early years with our older-adopted girls, that thought popped into my head pretty often. I kept pushing it away, though, determined that the next thing I tried would finally be the magic ticket to family happiness. We tried to motivate the kids in so many ways: reward charts and chores and time-outs and lost outings and on and on. But I didn't understand until later that all those ideas come from the same correction-based parenting paradigm. It's how John and I were both parented, and as I said earlier, it worked well with most of our kids. But it took years to face the fact that rewards and consequences were failing our kids from hard places.

We weren't alone in getting stuck there for a while. If it's all you know, what else is there to do? Not giving a consequence for disobedience can feel like you're not truly addressing the problem, or that your kid is getting away with defiance and not learning a thing. In fact, there are Christians who see "the rod" as *the* biblical way to handle defiance.

Yes, there are scriptures that talk about the rod of correction. But remember, the rod is the tool of a shepherd, and it is most often used to guide. And to get true perspective on the rod, we really need to read more of what the Bible has to say about the relationship between a shepherd and his sheep.

"My sheep hear My voice, and I know them, and they follow Me" (John 10: 27 NKJV). (Our kids won't follow us until they *know* us!)

"He will feed his flock like a shepherd. He will carry the lambs in his arms, holding them close to his heart. He will gently lead the mother sheep with their young" (Isa. 40:11 NLT). (Isn't it lovely to read that our Shepherd knows that mothers and their lambs need special nurturing?)

"The LORD is my shepherd; I shall not want. He makes me to lie down in green pastures. He leads me beside the still waters. He restores my soul; He leads me in the paths of righteousness for His name's sake. Yea, though I walk through the valley of the shadow of death, I will fear no evil; for You are with me; *Your rod and Your staff, they comfort me*" (Ps. 23:1–4 NKJV, emphasis added). (Anyone need comfort and soul restoration today? Our Shepherd is the source!)

As parents it is certainly our job to guide and correct and lead our children. We need to address behavior issues and show them how to be God honoring and respectful. And sometimes that will also mean giving consequences for wrong behavior. But we've got to *start* by building relationship, to help our children learn the sound of our voices and begin to trust our intentions for them.

It can be really tempting to see behaviors as *the* problem. But behaviors are just the symptoms, reminding us of the walls in our kids' hearts. What built those walls? Trauma. Fear. Loss.

Harsh, punitive corrections like spanking are only going to build walls higher in their hearts. We need to begin with gentleness and connection, with relationship building, to get our children hearing our voices. For some children this process takes years, taking down tall walls brick by brick so we can find the real child behind the walls.

One thing that John and I didn't realize at first (and still need to remind ourselves *often)* is that fear looks exactly like rebellion. Fearful kids are desperate to control their surroundings to protect themselves. And the more fearful they are, the more they will try to control. (Adults do this too: when kids' choices make us fearful, don't we often react by overcontrolling?) Problem is, if we see only our kids' rebellion and forget the fear underneath, we're going to get frustrated and tend to be much too harsh with consequences. Remember, it is God's kindness that leads us to repentance.

We've got to remember that most of our kids in a very real way are brokenhearted. Carissa Woodwyk (www.carissawoodwyk.word press.com), a family therapist who was adopted from Korea as an infant, said, "Children who were relinquished, who lost their parents, who experienced trauma or neglect or abuse . . . *they* were impacted by our broken world so early. The messages their hearts received from the enemy were distorted, untrue. It messed with them."[1]

So what does the Bible say about lovingly shepherding the brokenhearted?

- "The LORD is close to the brokenhearted and saves those who are crushed in spirit." (Ps. 34:18)

- "He heals the brokenhearted and binds up their wounds." (Ps. 147:3 NKJV)
- "But he was pierced for our transgressions; he was crushed for our iniquities; *upon him was the chastisement that brought us peace*, and with his wounds we are healed." (Is. 53:5 ESV, emphasis added)

Think about what Jesus did for the sinners around Him. He ate dinner with them. He sat and spoke with them when others shunned them. He forgave and healed and loved. Yes, He spoke law at times. But when a young ruler walked away from Him, grieved because Jesus had just asked him to give up his baggage (his riches), Jesus didn't tackle him and pry his riches out of his hands. He let him go. And then He spread out His arms and died for us all.

More and more I've come to understand that adoptive parents are in a very real way called to the cross to help our children heal. Yes, that cross is painful. It is hard to show grace and humility and gentleness to wounded ones who are reaching out to hurt us too, who aren't ready to give up their fear and begin to trust, who are showing that fear through rebellion. It's hard to love without getting anything back.

It's the most human thing in the world to want to punish, to inflict pain. But when we do that, we lose sight of how desperately we all need grace in our lives. How it is His kindness that leads us to repentance. How much we owe our Savior. How grateful we should be for grace.

And here's the other problem with consequences. Consequences work on the assumption that a child's core belief about herself is positive and therefore she will choose good things for herself. Many adopted children deep down see themselves as flawed humans who were given away because they were bad. A child who believes he's bad will expect more bad things to happen to him, and will often behave in a way that guarantees more bad things will happen. A child who has been hurt by loved ones will expect hurt from everyone else too. In fact, often they become master button pushers, goading parents to the limits, determined to prove that their perceptions of the world are true.

I spent years trying to use logic with my hurting kids to get them to do the right thing, assuming that they would choose good for themselves. Instead, I got behavior that sometimes looked downright incomprehensible. Dr. Karyn Purvis, speaking to adoptive families at a conference I attended, said, "Sad kids act angry and scared kids act crazy."[2] She added that the most difficult behavior comes from the need to look into our Father's face and be known and accepted just as we are. But here's the million-dollar question: How can we address difficult behavior while still clearly holding out that love to our children and showing them how precious they are to us?

What Not to Do

In her work with adoptive families, Debra Delulio Jones, the founder of Parenting Adoptees Can Trust (www.parentingadoptees cantrust.com), saw parents making errors repetitively in the same types of ways. She described those errors in a training session she did for parents at the Orphan Summit in 2013.[3] Parents with very anxious or volatile children sometimes become so worn out that they become overly permissive just to avoid a blow-up. Jones told the story of a child who became so agitated when anyone else flushed a toilet that, to avoid daily meltdowns, her family allowed her to be in charge of all toilet-flushing in the home. Thankfully, with some trust-based parenting strategies, the child is making great progress and now anyone in the family can flush a toilet without fear of a meltdown.

Other families, not realizing how profoundly their kids have been affected by trauma, have expectations that are too high and become too punitive. (Raising my hand here.) Another thing that parents often do is use too many words when correcting. (Me again.) We can also get into the habit of using disapproving looks and body language, something that almost always triggers the child's fight-or-flight reflex. Correcting a child who's in fight or flight is yet another common mistake parents make, not realizing that a freaked-out kid is a kid who's not hearing a thing we say. (Yup, me again. Suffice it to say, this was a very humbling list for me to read. No wonder we had some bumpy years, despite all my good intentions.)

Dr. Karyn Purvis, in her book *The Connected Child*, described ideal parenting for wounded children as high structure and high nurture. Kids need limits. But they also need huge amounts of nurture. As mentioned earlier, a ratio of five yes answers to every no is about right. Remember that infant in his mother's arms, and all the thousands of unconditional yes answers he gets? "Yes, I'll feed you. Yes, I'll pick you up. Yes, I'll soothe you." It goes on and on and on.

With an older child who is struggling with behavior issues, it can be incredibly difficult to get in that healing yes-to-no ratio. But with some creativity it can be done, and meeting needs over and over is an essential part of building connections. Only after we've met needs repetitively and begun to build trust can we correct effectively.

At an adoption conference I attended in Austin, Texas, in 2010, Purvis said, "If you can tuck that child under your wing, you can usually get him to come with you." But what does this look like in real life? As it turns out, a lot like 1 Corinthians 13:4–8: "Love is patient, love is kind. It does not envy, it does not boast, it is not proud. It does not dishonor others, it is not self-seeking, it is not easily angered, it keeps no record of wrongs. Love does not delight in evil but rejoices with the truth. It always protects, always trusts, always hopes, always perseveres. *Love never fails*" (emphasis added).

Addressing Misbehavior While Remaining Connected

Any time we need to address a misbehavior, it's important to begin by seeing and addressing the feelings that lead to our kids' misbehavior. Our kids are sinners, just like we are, and desperately need guidance and limits. Sometimes there may need to be consequences, chances to redo hard moments correctly or to make restitution for the wrong things they did to someone else. But they need to know we care about their feelings and that we love them no matter what.

When a kid goes into downstairs-brain (fight-or-flight) thinking, it's crucial *not* to go there ourselves. We can't lead our kids to a more regulated state than we are in ourselves. We need to *be* the calm that they so desperately need in their hard moments. We need to think of ways to creatively, lovingly meet their needs while still honoring God with appropriate boundaries on behaviors. This means speaking in a gentle voice, using soft eyes and loving words, and empathizing with their feelings *first* before going into how they should handle a similar moment in the future. If they're not ready to talk right away, we may just need to sit nearby, waiting for calm to return, reminding them that they're safe and we're there.

Calm isn't always easy to find, for kids or for parents. It can be hugely challenging to regulate our own emotions in the thick of difficult parenting, and sometimes we may sound aggressive or unloving without even realizing it. I struggle to keep my cool when we're running late and a child's misbehavior derails my agenda. Realizing that's a hard time for me has helped, but still I have to remind myself that the people in front of me are more important than the clock ticking on my wrist.

When do you struggle? Record some casual conversation around the dinner table and really listen to how you sound. Warm and nurturing? Or bossy and judgmental? Look at yourself in the mirror sometime when you're angry to get an idea of how you appear to your children. Would you be drawn to that person?

This kind of parenting is hard work, and none of us are going to do it perfectly. We're all going to need to apologize to kids at times, and to give ourselves grace for being human and making mistakes. But willingness to assess ourselves honestly is important so that we can give the Holy Spirit humble, fertile ground on which to work.

Relationship Destroyers:
judgment, harshness, unfair treatment, being controlling, anger, condemnation, shortness, overreacting, bitterness, self-pity, nonacceptance

Relationship Builders:
love, understanding, patience, kindness, gentleness, acceptance, peacefulness, honesty, affection, laughter, humor, conversation, listening, taking interest

Tools to Remember

1. Time in, *not* time out. Sometimes a frazzled mom or an angry teen may need some time apart to regain calm. But in general it is best to bring children closer rather than sending them away when they are upset. When it is necessary to give a consequence, ask yourself if that consequence is distancing or connecting. It is better for the relationship to make choices that will give you opportunities to build relationship, rather than being isolated from each other.

2. With young children, gently use your body to stop problem behavior. Physically moving a child to a different location is more effective than commanding him from across the room. If your child is reaching for a forbidden item, move the child or the item. Be gentle but firm when stopping a child from hitting, kicking, or hurting. Back up your action with simple, calm words. Obviously this takes time and a willingness to remain calmly, physically present even as you remind children of the boundaries on their behavior. For children too old to be physically moved toward obedience, it often helps just to sit nearby reading or doing something quiet with another child as you wait for the child to calm down enough to talk about a problem behavior. I find praise music tremendously calming during hard moments.

3. Aim for resolution. When a child makes a mistake, don't take it personally. Get close. Touch her gently under her chin and ask for eye contact. Communicate rules simply using only a handful of words at a time. You

can also ask her if she'd like a compromise, or suggest that she choose between two options that you can live with. Options like this encourage her to calm down and use her thinking brain.

4. Offer redos. Once a child has calmed down, give him a chance to redo the interaction in the correct way. That builds neural pathways for correct behavior in the future. Be willing to compromise, but keep asking for connection. Say, "Would you like a redo?" Teach kids how to communicate their frustrations respectfully. Then listen. And if something jumps out of your child's mouth that he immediately regrets—haven't we all had that happen?—give him a chance to redo the interaction and repair the damage.

5. Remind them you're on their side. Focus on the child's value as a child of God instead of on the failure. Struggling kids desperately need to hear that they are valuable and precious, aside from their performances or lack of them. Hug. Praise small successes. Say, "How can I help you right now?" And don't be surprised if some days are just plain hard despite your best effort.

6. Set them up for success. Discuss situations ahead of time. Talk through right behavior in the grocery store, or the proper way to clean a bedroom, or the right way to tell Grandma thanks for the birthday gift. For example, "I'm going to ask you to clean your room. Can you show me the wrong way to answer Mom? Can you show me a halfway good answer? Okay, now let's try having you show me the right way." If your child is resistant to this type of conversation, try role-playing a situation with

puppets, or let the child be the mom and you be the child, doing things the right way and the wrong way. This can be fun and bonding, especially if you pick a moment when the child is calm and approach the role-play with humor.

7. Say yes as often as you can. At times some of my kids seem to be experts at asking questions that will force me to say no, almost like they feel most comfortable with me denying them things. But really, they desperately need to hear yes. So I've gotten really creative at saying yes even in moments where yes is not the obvious answer. If a child asks me for a cookie when I am minutes from serving dinner, I'll say, "Yes, put it next to your plate to eat after you finish your dinner." If they want to watch a movie or stay up late, I'll say, "Sure, let's do that Friday night." If my teen asks to go sky diving or to go on a road trip across the USA or to buy a motorcycle or a semiautomatic rifle (yes, these are all real questions mine have asked), I'll say, "Sure, when you're a grown-up." Even though the real meaning of that answer is wait, hearing the word *yes* is a powerful thing. Recently I sneaked in a yes with an older teen by giving her a few extra minutes on Facebook on a night that I really would have preferred she finish her homework. The payoff came that very evening, when she came and snuggled next to me on the couch. Sure, she used the moment to sigh over her homework, but to have *her* initiate the communication and connection was a tremendous encouragement to this weary momma who's been trying so hard for so long. We really *are* getting somewhere. Praise God!

8. Look for patterns. If you're having trouble figuring out what tends to cause your child to melt down, try keeping a journal for a week or two. When did hard moments happen? What do you think is driving the behavior? What was your response? What were the results? Often you can figure out your child's trigger points and either talk her through the anxiety, or come up with a way to help that situation feel less stressful in the first place.

One daughter and I were repeatedly having issues first thing in the morning. Thinking it through, I realized we were both contributing. She comes out half awake and not ready for interaction. I come out (as always) longing for a bit of cheery interaction that will reassure me there's hope for a good day together. Instead, she snarls. I ask for a redo. She snarls again. And we're off. Not in a good way.

It's really hard for me to release that longing for pleasant interaction and not to address her disrespect. But at this point in her life, she's not strong enough to do that first thing in the morning. And, so as an act of love, I'm (mostly) choosing to be the pleasant greeter who then quickly walks past pretending not to notice the sour face and the lack of an answer. If rudeness happens after she's had a chance to wake up, I gently address it and ask for a redo. But I'm choosing not to go there first thing in the morning.

Yes, in a way I am giving up. I am giving up on a small goal in hope of someday attaining a greater goal: the growth of a relationship that is more likely to happen if I can resist reacting to small indignities. "I have been crucified with Christ; and it is no longer I who live, but Christ lives in me; and the life which I now live in the flesh I live by faith in the Son of God, who loved me and gave Himself for me" (Gal. 2:20 NKJV).

Spirals in Small Moments

I mentioned before that when kids first arrive, there tends to be a spiral either in an upward or a downward direction. Upward or downward spirals can happen in smaller ways too, within interactions on a daily basis. The other day when preparing to let a teen go someplace, I laughingly said, "You'll behave, right?" totally expecting a quick reassurance.

"Nope!" was the quick reply. My child laughed too, but the tone was sassy. Since a friend was there, I let the child save face and laughed along, thinking we'd talk later about that tone. After thinking through my irritation, I realized that though I truly had reasonable confidence in my child's good intent, I really *had* wanted to hear that reassurance out loud. Instead, the snide sass and the child's refusal to reassure me triggered anxiety in me, more than I even knew I had over the outing.

Okay, so that bit was my junk, but why had my child responded that way? Just to irritate me? Sometimes I'm quick to assume that, but I realized in this case it might be that *my* question had triggered frustration in my teen—the "why doesn't Mom trust me?" variety. Thus, the sass.

So instead of a lecture, the way I decided to address the little snafu was with an apology. I told my teen that I'd asked the question just wanting to hear a reassurance, but realized afterward that the question had felt insulting, and I was sorry.

If I'd gone into that talk all guns firing, lecturing about rudeness, we'd have had WW3 in an instant. Instead, at my apology, my teen's face went completely contrite, and my child instantly apologized as well. Because I'd actually managed to read the situation correctly and then apologized for my part in it, the interaction ended with a warmth and connection and a lightness that was truly wonderful. Sometimes I make such wrong assumptions in the midst of conflict, and the situation spirals downward in seconds. But, wow, it is worth it to puzzle through challenging moments and figure out what might be distressing both me *and* my child.

Helpful Phrases for Hard Moments[4]

Phrases followed by an asterisk were adapted from *Empowered to Connect 'Life Scripts'* by Dr. Karyn Purvis.

- "Listen and obey,"* or "Who's in charge?"* (Encourages respect of authority.)
- "Are you asking or telling?"* (Encourages respectful communication.)
- "Use your words,"* or "Give me good words and eyes."* (Encourages appropriate communication.)
- "Try that again with respect,"* or "Would you like a redo?"* (Gives child practice doing it right. Might need to wait until child is calm to ask for redo.)
- "When you've done _____, then you may _____." (Clearly connects obedience with a privilege that the child has just requested.)
- "Either do _____ or _____." (Clearly connects an action with a consequence if they decide not to obey.)

- "Is it a big problem or a little one?" (Helps kids take a deep breath and get perspective.)
- "How can I help you?" or "What do you need?" (Gives you a chance to say yes to your child.)
- "Do you want to _____ by yourself or with my help?"* (Obedience isn't optional, but child can decide if he needs help.)
- "This is just a small problem, but . . ." (Avoids triggering the fight-or-flight response.)
- "I have to tell you something I know you are not going to like." (Prepares child for a hard moment, which often helps her react less extremely.)
- "I care about you, and I wonder what's going on that has you feeling so upset." (Shows concern.)
- "Asked and answered." (Short response when a child is repeatedly asking the same question.)

You Can . . .

Staci (www.scoopingitup.blogspot.com), a mom with several older-adopted children, has found the words "you can . . ." to be very useful: "Kids with special needs, and even neuro-typical ones don't know what to say or do much of the time. So they act badly, speak rudely, and panic that they will not be heard or have their needs met. One of my kiddos, new to English, new to family life, new to making decisions and thinking about anything at all, really, *does not know what to do* a lot of the time. While an excellent follower, if the other children are absent, given the opportunity to make a choice on how to act or what to say, this child flounders, freezes. I have to put on my therapist hat [and] pretend this child is like her far younger toddler brothers.

> You can say, 'Thanks for the apple, Mom.'
> You can take your plate to the sink.
> You can read for a few minutes.
> You can tell the truth.
> You can say sorry.
> You can look at my eyes.
> You can say, 'What time are we going?'
> I said it's time to get in the car, so you can drop the puzzle and put on shoes.
> You can tell your friend, 'Thank you for coming!'

"The difference between commanding, 'Say sorry to your brother!' and 'You can say sorry' is subtle and makes a larger impact. All of a sudden the child has options."

Recognize and Steer Clear of Emotional Tornadoes

Once a young teen was upset because I'd told her that a library book she selected wasn't okay to read. We set it aside, but when it came time to gather books to return to the library, she began venting her irritation over my choice in a resentful tone of voice. "Where's that book you said I can't read? Now I have to return it, and it was the most interesting one I picked, and you had to say no just because [adult sister] didn't like one little thing . . ."

Without even thinking, I reacted, matching her tone with an equally cranky one of my own. "There's a good reason she said that book was not okay. You're just going to have to trust that I have your best interests in mind."

A second later I realized I'd just been sucked into downstairs-brain thinking right along with her. My irritation was not really about the book. It was about a trigger of mine: her ongoing lack of trust in my good intent. She was assuming, again, that I was being mean, when really I was acting in love.

But blowing up because of it was not going to help. I took a deep breath and started again. "Wait a second," I said, willing myself to speak softly. "I'm sorry I yelled at you just then. That wasn't what I meant to do. Here's the deal: when Amanda looked at it the other day, she found sex scenes in the book."

All anger dropped off my daughter's face. She flushed. "Oh."

I went on gently. "That's why I said no. I'm really not trying to ruin your fun. I just think there's better stuff for you to read. Okay?"

"Okay," she sighed, except now her face was soft, like she actually saw the sense in my decision. And we were able to move on, both of us now better regulated. If I'd lectured her longer, or even quit talking after my first impatient response, she'd still have been mad. But by taking a breath, choosing the high road, apologizing for my anger, and then explaining the decision gently, I was able to lead her into better regulation of her own emotions.

Of course, to be able to do that, I first had to realize I was being triggered and regulate my own response. So hard. Too often I convince myself that my frustration is justified. But I can't lead my child someplace I haven't been myself. To help my children heal and begin to regulate their own emotions, I have to begin by taking control of the ones raging in my own head. Being willing to apologize also has tremendous power to touch our children's hearts.

Elizabeth Curry (www.ordinary-time.blogspot.com) is the mother of ten children, some of whom struggle with mood regulation. "It is typical of a dysregulated, struggling child to want to hijack the good times a family is sharing with an eye to making everyone as miserable as the hurt child is feeling. And they are very, very good at this. It takes a lot of practice and a lot of grace to be able to ignore the behavior of the child and focus on the rest of the family. But my other children need to experience good family times too. . . . The only way I [can] do this is by God's power and grace."

Step Away When You Get Stuck

There will be times when you may need to be willing to wait for obedience, or to reframe your expectations to make your request doable for a child. Sometimes my teens are so deep in downstairs-brain thinking that nothing good is going to come from further interaction at that moment. It's a hugely valuable skill to realize they're stuck and to be able to step back and say, "It's not okay that you're refusing to obey, but we'll talk about this again another time."

If after a reasonable cooling-off time for both parties, the child is still stuck, it's okay to gently restate the request, make it clear obedience needs to happen, then move on. Eventually they'll probably want something from you badly enough that they will decide to obey.

Once, one of my daughters was dysregulated and utterly refused to answer me respectfully. In the past, I would have been intent on ending the conflict immediately. I certainly would have yelled and probably grounded her and taken away other privileges. The end result might have been physical obedience, but it would not have built any kind of trust, and the consequences would still be playing out long after that particular incident was over. (Ideally consequences should not drag on for weeks after a misdeed.)

So this time I used some newfound skills. First, I recognized that she was triggered and so wasn't able at that moment to use her upstairs brain. Second, I realized her defiance was triggering me, which let me take a deep breath, stay calm, and *keep* using my upstairs brain. And third, I told her that she could wait to obey until she was strong enough to obey, but she would eventually still need to obey. Giving her outright permission to take some time took some of the frustration out of it for me.

Then, thankfully, it was bedtime. Every momma has her limits, after all.

The next morning her mood hadn't improved. I told her she would need to stay in the same room I was in until she decided to obey. She was sour but compliant with small things I asked her to do during the day. When it was time to go to youth group with the other teens, I told her she was welcome to go if she was ready to obey. She wasn't.

I continued to interact with her in a pleasant way, deliberately ignoring many little distancing things she was doing during this time. Oh, she wanted me to be angry with her. But by God's grace,

I still was able to continue to love her. Finally, the next morning she decided to obey. And the angels sang. It was the very first time that such huge defiance from her had ended with me steadily showing love instead of getting angry. And still, in the end, she obeyed.

I am hoping that eventually she will begin to see and feel my love more clearly, begin to trust, and want to be more respectful to me. But whether or not I get the desired result, staying calm is helping me love her more like Jesus.

Not perfectly—there are still plenty of moments when steam begins to waft from my ears and I have to take a deep breath and say a prayer, moments where my words aren't quite as gentle as I wish. Moments for which I need to apologize. But overall I am going to bed at night happier with myself, and more certain that no matter the end result, I'm giving this relationship my best. For Jesus.

TWENTY-MINUTE FIXES FOR A HARD DAY

- Read a psalm out loud at the beginning of a meal, and pray for God's peace for your family. His word will not return void.
- Turn on praise music and sing along. Praising God will boost your mood, and it will speak hope to your child, perhaps even more than just music in the background.
- Go for a walk with your kids. Breathe deeply. Look up at the sky. Admire the leaves. If it's raining, dance in the rain even if you get soaking wet. If it's hot, have a Popsicle afterward. If it's cold, make cocoa, or roast mini marshmallows over a candle at the

kitchen counter. You'll make memories your kids will never forget.

- Clean something. Scrub hard. Make it look better. There. You've improved a corner of your world. Don't you feel better?

- Throw away twenty-seven things. Tell your kids to throw away some of their junk too. Sort it into throw-away and give-away piles. Enjoy the extra breathing room in your home.

Begin as You Want to Continue?

Kate and her husband are experienced parents who adopted a little boy from Ethiopia when he was six. "We had heard the oft-repeated advice of 'begin as you will continue' when adopting older children, and we took it to heart. I was absolutely paralyzed by the idea that any bad behaviors we let slip would be absolutely entrenched forevermore. One night my new son refused to sit down to eat his dinner. He did the Ethiopian finger wag and said firmly, 'Abi no sit.'

"My heart froze. How could I let him stand at the dinner table? I had to act quickly or this would escalate; I was certain of it. I took his dinner and *refused* to let him eat until he was sitting. Strong willed and stubborn, he would not eat that night, and simply stood there while the rest of us had our dinner. The next night, sure enough, he sat. But did I really win that battle? And if so, at what cost?

"Thinking back now, I wish I had not taken that early advice so seriously and concretely. Yes, I think parents should 'begin as they will continue' in the sense that if you do not generally buy your kids everything they want at Target, or let them stay up until midnight watching movies, or buy junky cereals, etc., then you should not introduce those behaviors early on. But I'm not so sure about the other stuff. Maybe I should have let Abi eat standing up that night. He had been through an incredible trauma and now he was in a new house in a new country with a new language and a new family, and if eating standing up gave him one little ounce of control over his life, was it really necessary for me to break that will? There were literally hundreds more such incidents over the months (fine, years) to follow.

"If I had it to do again (ah, hindsight!) I would have put more emphasis on the big picture stuff—kindness to siblings and others, cooperation in the family, respectful language—and less on the minutiae—on the following through of every single rule. I would have spent more time on loving my new little guy, and less on being so fearful that I was going to lose control if I let anything at all slide. Maybe better advice for parents adopting older kids would be 'stay flexible, and pick your battles.'"

When Kids Push You Away

There are so many ways that kids push moms away. Each time it happens, it hurts, and we are left trying to figure out how to handle their behavior while also feeling our own hurt. One mom I spoke with was distressed because after she'd spent hours braiding her daughter's hair, the daughter would undo her braids or put sand in her hair. Those of you familiar with curly hair are shuddering with me, right? Sand is a nightmare in curls. This frustrated momma asked what she could do to discourage this behavior.

I think first we've got to remember that actions are only symptoms of deeper feelings. Maybe the child doesn't feel comfortable being nurtured. Maybe she has memories of her first mom doing her hair and it's just too painful to share this time with a new mom.

Here's a similar example. Some of my kids *love* coffee in the morning, and sometimes when they're feeling prickly I'll offer them a cup as a way to love them a little. When they're well regulated, my offer is usually met with a grin—coffee is not an everyday treat for kids around here. But there have been times when kids have refused a steaming hot cup of creamy sweetness, just because they detect the nurture I'm trying to sneak in along with the caffeine and sugar. And they don't want any.

I think the biggest (and hardest) thing to do then is to be non-reactive, to show love, and a little later to gently talk through their feelings. In the case of the little girl with the sandy hairdos, I'd probably skip labor-intensive styles for a while too. But what we can't do is let our frustration stop us from nurturing.

Kids' behavior is the worst when their most vulnerable feelings are closest to the surface. An aggressive or out-of-control child is a stressed child, one who desperately needs sensitive caring from an adult. It may help to think of misbehavior as similar to a physical illness. Instead of dreading the next offense, see it as a chance to nurture your child and (eventually) talk about his feelings.

One day recently one of my children was being exceedingly oppositional. All morning long she responded to my overtures rudely, and over and over again I gently asked her to redo her responses with respect. Now and then she'd get mad enough to outright refuse to cooperate in any way, so I'd have her lie down on the couch near me to "rest until you feel strong enough to obey."

Though I felt pretty provoked at times, I managed to stay calm and warm all morning. Wash, rinse, repeat, staying chill. I even managed to chat cheerily with some of the other kids while the challenging child was having time-in next to me on the couch. The whole morning she was basically dysregulated, with some better time in the afternoon, and then more dysregulation in the evening. She gave me *lots* of chances to practice loving responses to defiance. It was such a hard day, and I wasn't sure if I'd made any long-term impact on her behavior. But I went to bed feeling confident that I'd shown her lots of nurturing while still insisting on respect.

The next morning I came out of my bedroom fully expecting more of the same. But lo and behold, she was pure gold. All day long. Chatty, sweet, offering information, even smiling into my eyes. It was so very unusual and so good. Several times throughout that day I felt off balance during an interaction where she continued to speak and interact, long past the point where she usually clammed up. I am hoping that as I get better at this gentle style of parenting, we'll get more of both kinds of days—hard ones where I am successful in loving responses, and maybe even some sweet ones now and then.

Christie M. (http://parentingthatheals.org/) wrote, "I think so many times we are on a mission to 'fix' our children. We are on the fast track to make them whole, and in the process, we may be missing God's timing, and our children's timing. They may not be ready for things to be discussed. They may just need to chill and be loved just for who they are, with all their quirks and unpacked bags. . . . But in God's timing, it will happen. God's timing evokes change from the heart. It is welcomed and does not bring resentfulness and anger. His timing brings about repentance and healing. If it were up to me, I'd want everything fixed today. No, YESTERDAY! But God is multilayered. He knows that I need to continue to learn patience and kindness and a big helping of MORE forgiveness. And as He helps them unpack their bags, He shows me that I still have some bags to unpack too, and so we do it together."

Keeping Perspective, Having Faith

One morning a year or two ago, I stood in the garden, cranky over two rows of corn that I thought had been weeded two days ago.

"Dad told us to come inside because it was raining," my teens told me, and I was fine with that, except that (again) they didn't tell me what was going on. Hello, trigger. "Next time just tell me when you come inside, okay? I just want to know what's going on."

Eyes rolled. "Didn't you hear the thunder that day, Mom? Why should we have to tell you? We don't have to tell you everything."

Me and my unreasonable requests for communication. And it was just weeds. But it was not just weeds. It was relationship. It was communication. I'd been loving them for many long years, and darn it, that day I was hurting because it felt like I was still not worth five sentences to them. The hurt stabbed deep. "Just talk to me," I said. "That's what moms and kids do. Do you know how much I want you to talk to me?"

"We talked to you about church camp the other day!" one retorted, indignant, sure I was overreacting.

I remembered the conversation, where I'd asked twenty questions for a few hard-won phrases. "Yeah, I'm glad you answered my questions. Really. But I'd love it if you'd talk to me sometimes when it's your idea. Just come sit by me on the couch and tell me something. Anything."

We pulled weeds and argued, the conversation plowing familiar hard ground, and I was so darn sad that I didn't care if the neighbor heard the wail in my voice. I was so very sad. Sad from years of being pushed away. That day they told me straight out they were just biding their time.

"I'm leaving as soon as I can," said one. "I'm not coming back."

"We're not happy here," said another. "Don't you know that?"

Never mind all the good in their lives; at that moment they didn't see a speck of it. And you know what, at that moment, I didn't either.

─────

It was another day that same summer. Again we were in the garden, this time picking green beans, harvest from our earlier work. Somehow the kids and I got on the topic of me as an old lady. The very kid who'd just weeks earlier threatened to go away and never come back looked me in the eye and said, "I might be able to take care of you when you're old."

And my heart melted in a puddle and angels sang over my head. Once again I was reminded that I can't let myself be dragged down by words spoken in anger. Oh, I've let myself be dragged into the pit of despair at times. Despair that leaves me fearing for the future. But feelings are temporary.

Feelings, both ours and our kids', are *temporary*.

Keep breathing, keep waiting, keep hoping. Not in our children, but in our only true hope: the perfect, all-sufficient love of Jesus. Our hope is in the Lord and in His unfailing promises. Feelings are temporary. Jesus is eternal. Halleluiah!

Carol, a mother of fifteen children, knows the challenge of loving a child who doesn't yet know how to give back. "The first full English sentence that my four-year-old said was, 'I want you to die so I can be the mom.' Not something you want to write in the memory book. My daughter has Down syndrome, though, and struggled with English. So honestly, my first thought was, *That was a really long and well-framed sentence!* Her statement just put into words exactly what she had been telling me by her behavior."

Love Is an Action Verb

These days folks usually think *love* equals all sorts of sweet, heart-tugging feelings. Sometimes that's true. But most of all love is about action. In fact, doing what is good and right toward a person who is actively rejecting you may actually be *more* loving (and is certainly harder) than the easy kind of love that we tend to feel for kids who give us all sorts of positive feedback. We rarely realize how much of our responses toward the "easy" people in our lives is simply an instinctive, reciprocal thing. Yes, it is a beautiful feedback loop, a gift from God. But it doesn't happen just because our feelings are "right" toward those people. It happens partly because the other people are doing their half of that sweet back-and-forth game.

When we are loving a person who isn't giving us that positive feedback, it feels hard because we're trying to hold up both sides of the relationship ourselves. When relationships are hard, we as mommas often feel guilty and conclude we're not loving well enough. We'd do better to simply acknowledge the difference and keep on loving anyway, with eyes fixed on Jesus, the Author and Perfecter of our faith.

Real love isn't always touchy-feely sweetness. Real love is putting a twinkle in your eye and giving a hug to a little rebel. Because he needs it whether he knows it or not. Real love is seeing past the smart mouth and admiring the dimples, then asking the child for a redo with a smile. Real love is taking a stab at guessing the feelings of a kid who honestly has no idea what she's feeling, and then hugging her when she shoots down every single idea you suggest.

Real love is combing his hair. Real love is finding her an adorable outfit to wear today. Or reminding yourself that she looks beautiful even in that ratty gray sweatshirt that you hate. Real love is snuggling, and tickling, and kissing their faces. Or sometimes not hugging them when you want to because that's what they prefer. Real love is choosing to act in a loving way toward someone because of the commitment we've made. And often *practicing* real love day by day also leads eventually to all those squeezy-heart feelings we were hoping for in the first place.

Sometimes healing is big and quick and dramatic and thorough. Sometimes it just means chipping away, loving without obvious impact. Keep the pace of life slow. Take time to rest, time to recharge in the Word. The fact that God entrusted these children to us means that He thinks we're the right ones for the task. It's some of the hardest, most meaningful work we'll ever do.

Steady on, have faith. With His help and His grace and His wisdom, we can do this job well. Remember that our worth as a precious child of God is not dependent upon our apparent success or failure as mommas. And our children's choices, good or bad, don't change their worth either. Keep affirming their goodness and value, speaking to them of hope. "This behavior is only a small bit of you. I know there's good in you. Right now, even in this hard moment, He is speaking to your heart and making you new." And he is making us new too, isn't He?

Forgetting what is behind and straining
toward what is ahead,
I press on toward the goal to win the prize
for which God has called me heavenward in Christ Jesus.
PHILIPPIANS 3:13–14

CHAPTER 9

In Their Words:
Thoughts from Adoptees

In June of 2009, I was once again hugging my husband good-bye at the airport. This time I was headed for South Korea with three of our sons: Josh and Ben, our Korean-born sons, both eleven at the time, and Daniel, then fifteen. John and I wanted Josh and Ben to have some memories of their own of Korea, and we'd been planning a homeland visit for quite a while. After corresponding with the social workers at Ben's adoption agency in Korea, we'd found out that Ben's birth family was eager to meet him.

Though Ben had initially been very positive about the idea, as we flew toward Korea, I could see nervousness creeping in. Josh outright said he was glad he wasn't meeting his own family. I felt anxious too. Oh, I hoped this meeting would be good for our boy.

Once in Korea, we were blessed to be shown around by the niece of an Idaho friend who'd moved from Korea to America in her twenties. We had a blessing-filled week shopping and sight-seeing and seeing Josh's and Ben's foster moms, who were both delighted to see the boys grown so big and doing so well.

Finally, just a few days before we flew back to America, it was time to meet with Ben's family. As we walked into the room at the adoption agency, my chest was tight. His mother was immediately standing, crying, embracing him, stroking his hair, touching his face, drinking in the sight of him. His dad stood back, face stern, tears welling, letting his wife greet their son first. Her grief was so great that I was instantly weeping as well, patting her back and telling her thank you over and over. The social worker guided everyone to sit, and it was then that Ben's dad pulled a chair close to Ben and sat down knee to knee, holding both of his hands and speaking earnestly.

Ben looked at me helplessly, knowing his dad was saying some-thing important but not understanding. The social worker jumped in to translate as the father apologized and shared more fully the reasons they were not able to parent him: it was a very difficult combination of unemployment, ill health, and Ben's medical needs. I'd always told him that their intentions for him were good. But seeing the emotion on their faces in person, watching how they stroked his cheek and smoothed his hair and examined his hands and sought out his eyes—oh, their love was so clear!

Ben was extremely shy at first—his father told him that shy-ness runs in the family—but answered their questions with a little coaxing from me. They were concerned about his health. I was quick to assure them that his prosthetic leg allows him to do any-thing that any other child can do. After an initial bit of visiting, we went together to a restaurant for lunch. All through the meal, his parents were filling his plate with choice morsels and encouraging him to eat and stroking his hair and studying his face.

His mother has a glowingly brilliant smile that often sparkled with tears. She was soaking up these moments. His father was more somber, his sadness more obvious. Yet there were delightful flashes of humor that reminded me so much of our son. Over and over again he reached out with warmth to Ben, talking to him, telling him how he resembled their family or explaining where he might have gotten some trait that they noticed.

By the end of the dinner, Ben was getting comfortable, joking and smiling more. I was so happy they were starting to see more of his true self. As the dinner wound down, no one wanted to say good-bye. The family asked if they could take us out for coffee. We walked to another place close by, sat in a little private space in a corner, and talked for another hour or so.

Finally the social worker gently suggested it was time to go. We were going to a baseball game at five—oh, how anticlimactic that sounded after all this—and his family had a three-hour train ride back home. We walked to the subway together, Ben walking alongside his dad with his dad's arm over his shoulders. I'll have that picture in my mind forever. Ben was peaceful, content—relieved, I think, that these strangers, his family, had turned out to be people of great kindness. But my heart ached hard for his parents, getting ready to say good-bye to their boy again.

We took more pictures, exchanged e-mail addresses, and agreed to try to come back to Korea in five years so that they could see Ben again. Good-byes were quietly tearful and put off for as long as possible, with many hugs, and his first mom and I took turns telling each other thank you. I kept waiting for them to turn and leave, but finally I realized that they couldn't tear themselves away. They couldn't leave him again. As the boys and I walked away, they watched tearfully, rooted to the spot, waving each time we looked back, wanting to hold on to every last instant of the sight of him. Oh, the sadness. My heart was broken wide open.

The boys seemed to feel the sadness less than I did. They chattered about how nice the family had been and how much fun it had been to meet with them. There was a lightness to Ben's face that hadn't been there in the day or two before the meeting—he was obviously relieved it had gone so well.

I could see a contentedness on Josh's face as well. Seeing the kindness of Ben's family made it easy to imagine that his family had similar good intent toward him. On the way home at the end of the trip, I asked the boys about their favorite part of the trip. Both quickly said that the very best part was meeting Ben's family. I would have to agree. Our hearts were full indeed.

When we go into adoption, we adoptive parents almost uniformly do it with the best intentions. We want another child, and love the idea of being family for a child who needs one. It seems so simple, so clearly good. But the deeper you get into adoption, the longer you are an adoptive family, the more you understand how others' losses are inescapably entwined with your own family's gain. Never was that pointed out to me more clearly than when meeting Ben's family.

But there've been other moments too. Not long ago, on the way home from a shopping trip with my teenage daughters, a song came on the radio, and one of the girls started singing along. She doesn't sing in the car all that often, and I drove along quietly, treasuring the sound of her happiness and thinking what a long time it had taken to get us here.

I remembered our second day together in Ethiopia, when John and I sat in on the evening worship in the orphanage. It was syncopated with energetic drumming done by a row of smiling girls pounding away on a wooden cupboard at the back of the room, two of whom were our daughters.

And then we brought the girls away from all they knew and came to Idaho, where we worship in a quiet Lutheran church where no one even raises their hands while praising God. Oh, how staid and dull that must have seemed after the raucous enthusiasm of Ethiopian worship.

The girls are used to it now, I think. They know the hymns and have favorite songs on Christian radio. One plays guitar. The other plays piano, mostly hymns, beautifully, and with feeling. I know they gained many good things by coming to America. But that hour of worship in Ethiopia gave me a tiny hint of what they lost when they came into our family. I don't ever want to forget that picture of my girls in the land of their birth, surrounded by friends, singing and drumming and praising God with great joy, because it helps me hold on more firmly to sympathy in hard moments.

Mothers Who See

Sometimes adoptive parents don't want to see that loss—they want to see it simply as another way to form a family. But it is far from simple, far from easy for the children. Adoption comes from great loss, as adoptees and their families will quickly tell us. If only we are brave enough to listen.

Mary (www.findingmagnolia.com) said, "We adopted our oldest daughter at the age of three and a half three years ago from

Ethiopia, and our youngest just one year ago. What has surprised me most is how much I wish I could change everything for my oldest in particular so she could have stayed in her first family. I knew I would feel that way before we adopted, but there's a huge difference between understanding the concept of loss and seeing its effects on my daughter, here in the flesh. She remembers her life before adoption and the process that brought her to our family quite clearly, and she misses her family in Ethiopia every day. Her struggles were huge in the beginning, and they still challenge her greatly."

Renee (www.steppinheavenward.blogspot.com) said, "I believe the greatest surprise to me is to know that there are times my children are going to hurt deeply over the losses in their lives and there is nothing I can do about it. I think as mothers we have this inherent need and compulsion to make things better. This is not a booboo we can kiss and heal with our words, a hug, and a smile. We have six sons through adoption. They came home between two and eight years ago. They are all doing well. Most days are great and they are fantastic kids. However, these moments creep up . . . sometimes days at a time, where they grieve.

"It can be set off by something seemingly benign or I can see it coming a mile away. One son goes through a spell every October. I have no idea what it is about October, and neither does he. Yesterday evening our son from China was playing with the little girl across the street and her sisters (it is a Chinese family) when I saw it in his face . . . sadness. He quietly slipped back into our home to go play alone.

"I have come to realize there is nothing I can do to fix it. I can sit with my children and mourn with them. I can listen. I can pray for them and over them. I can point them to the Healer of their souls. I in myself cannot fix it though, and I have had to release myself from that burden and conviction that I could, or even should. When Lazarus died and Jesus came to Mary and Martha and saw their grief, He wept. He felt their pain and understood the hurt that comes from being separated from loved ones. The Bible calls us to 'Rejoice with those who rejoice and mourn with those who mourn.' I have found my best response is to be with them, and listen to them, and sometimes just say nothing, but pray and hold on."

Nancy L. said, "I think that one of the biggest surprises for me about adoptive motherhood is learning that there can be multiple contradictory emotional truths for my daughter at any given time. She can be really happy and content in our family, and simultaneously have a sense of loss and sadness at the thought of the biological family she may never know. Even though these two things seem to contradict each other, they often coexist for my daughter. It is necessary for me to understand that her grief is not about me, and allow her to have whatever feelings she has—and it doesn't mean we have failed as her parents. [I want her to] feel free to talk about whatever she is feeling, and find that we are a safe haven for it all."

What Children Have to Say

Melanie's ten-year-old son Joseph had this to say about his new life: "I moved into my new home when I was seven and cried almost every night for a week because I was really afraid. I would only eat hot dogs with no bun and peanut butter and jelly sandwiches. Now I like to eat just about everything. I started homeschooling, and it was a lot better than it was to go to school. It helped me because I got to spend lots of time getting to know my four new brothers and sisters. My mom made me feel safe and told me I was going to be all right. Other people outside of my family told me right away that I was a perfect fit for my new family, and that made me happy. We live on a farm, and my parents let me have my own animals to take care of, which helped me be more responsible. When I wanted to be alone, I would spend time with my animals, and it helped me learn how to love better. Even though some things in my life were very hard, I trust in the Lord. He has a plan for me, and He loves me. My special Bible verse is Jeremiah 29:11: "'For I know the plans I have for you," says the Lord, "plans of peace and not of evil, to give you a future and a hope.'"

Casey said that her daughter came home at age five: "She remembered receiving a small photo album from us that could be attached by zip ties to her bed in Haiti. For the two and a half years she was waiting in the orphanage for us to complete the process, she kept the photo album safe; it was a precious item that belonged only to her. She said that the photo album was a big help to feel at home when she got here. She became familiar with our faces, her siblings' faces, and even our dog's face. She had practiced everyone's names from the labels we put with the pictures, and it was adorable to hear how she pronounced them all in her Kreyol accent. She said—in answer to a question about what she would want adoptive parents to know—that new parents need to remember that the kids aren't used to you and that it's okay if they're shy. It doesn't mean they don't like you; it just means they don't know you yet, and they might need some time on their own to just be shy."

Alyssa, who writes at www.mintflower.blogspot.com, has a son who was adopted from foster care at age seven. He had this to say about his adoption experience: "I was afraid they would be a bad family. I was a little bit scared, but not too scared. I did want a new mom and dad, but I was scared to see what color they were. I wanted to be white but I couldn't because God made me what I was. I thought maybe they wouldn't like my color.

"When I first got here, the best thing Mom and Dad did was take care of me in love. It was fun to cook pancakes and tortillas with Mom and play tickle with Dad. Parents should play games with their kids every day."

Hilary's girls came home at ten and half and eight and a half, and had been home for four years when she asked them questions about the early days home. She said the girls at first found it hard to call them Mom and Dad, and struggled to get used to the family rules. They also found it hard to eat different food. The girls said they enjoyed playing games, helping Mom cook meals, and helping Dad with car care (washing, changing oil, and rotating tires). The girls suggested that parents let children be involved in what they are doing, watch movies together, have family night, play games, and give equal attention to all the children. One daughter said that their kindness and love and godly actions drew her to her parents. "My advice would be give love notes and hugs and kisses and make them feel good in their house. Give them time to settle in their house. Talk about Jesus, who died for everyone because we all have sinned (Romans 3:23). Talk about their rules or tell them a story."

Hilary said, "Shortly after our girls came, I started telling them: 'You are safe, you are loved, you are wanted, and you belong.' I typed this up and posted it on their headboards for them to read whenever they wanted to. They have really appreciated those messages."

Marissa and her husband adopted Ephrem, Tsigerida, and Abiyu (a sibling group) from Ethiopia three years ago:

Ephrem said, "Adoption isn't easy for kids. You feel like you're from another planet. Anywhere you go, you're different from everyone else. It takes time for everything to get better."

Tsigerida had this to say: "Adoption is hard because your family are strangers. You have to get used to them being your parents. The language is hard. It's all different. It's like the world went upside down. It's good and bad, and it takes a long time to get used to everything."

Abiyu, the youngest, said this: "When you come into a new place and you're adopted, you don't know who's going to be there for you. I don't think I'm lucky to be adopted, but I think my parents are lucky to spend the rest of their lives with their children."

Ashley (www.ashleykwells.com) and her husband just finalized the adoption of a sibling group of four from the US foster care system.

She asked the oldest two children, nine-year-old Jonathan and six-year-old Jazmine, some questions about being adopted:

What is good about having your new family?

Jonathan: They love me and don't beat me and don't do drugs. They care about me and want me. They want to have fun with me.

Jazmine: It was good to have food and have parents that care about me. I get to play more.

What was hard?

Jonathan: I'm still sad that my old parents didn't stop doing drugs, and now I won't be able to see them again.

Jazmine: I cried because I missed my old mom and dad.

What did we do to make you feel connected to all of us?

Jonathan: My new mom and dad fed me every day, got me clothes to wear, they told me they loved me, they told me about God.

Jazmine: They fed me and tucked me in to bed every night.

Anything else you want to say about adoption and being adopted?

Jonathan: Adoption is awesome because I have a new family that loves me. I know this family is so much better, I'm so thankful that God chose this life for me.

Jazmine: I'm glad that I am here at my new house and I am glad I get to stay here forever. I like this place and this mom and dad.

Here's what my own daughter Julianna had to say about adoption. She is nine and came home at six months of age: "What's hard about being adopted is that you had to leave your first family. What's fun is coming to America and having a lot of friends and family here. I want to go back to Ethiopia and visit my first family.

But I have a bunch of brothers and sisters here, plus a brother and three sisters in Ethiopia. I love playing with my sister. My sisters [from Ethiopia] are my Ethiopian family in America, plus I have my Ethiopian family in Ethiopia. So my life is perfect, pretty much. Except sometimes I don't like being here and I say I want to go to Ethiopia, usually when I don't get my own way."

Adoption in the Words of Older Adoptees and Adults

Cyndi (www.lajoyfamily.blogspot.com) asked her daughter Angela, age fourteen (home for three years), to share some advice for parents adopting older children. Here are her wise words: "It's not a fairy tale, Mom. It's hard and uncomfortable, and everyone thinks it is going to be comfortable fast, but it won't be. You need to tell parents that it takes a lot longer than they think for everyone to feel like they are not strangers. They put too much pressure on themselves, maybe because they think everyone is watching them and they feel like they have to pretend they are all loving right away. That is silly; they can't be and no one should think they should be.

"Let your kids get mad at you, you don't have to be their best friend, you have to be their mom and dad. I won't forget on the airplane coming home when I was so rude to you, and you let me have it right there. I knew you were not someone to be that way with. I was MAD, but, Mom, if you hadn't done it then, I would have gotten worse and worse because I would have known you were scared to discipline me. Too many parents are too worried with their new kids that their kids will be mad at them and not love them, but what they are really doing is making it all harder by not being tough and loving parents right from the beginning.

"Tell parents this . . . tell them don't force their older kids to hug them and get too close to them. You and Dad did it just right, you played a lot with us. You gave us a lot of time and didn't expect us to be all huggy at first. You didn't push yourselves to us when we didn't really know you, you let us come give you hugs. But you know what I liked? You tried a little. Remember when at first I was really mean and cold to you, and pushed you away? You didn't force me to love you, and you didn't pretend it was all good. But you didn't act like you hated me either. And you would sneak in and put your arm around my shoulder sometimes or touch me on my hand or arm. At first—I don't want to hurt your feelings—but it felt really weird. I didn't think I liked it, because no one ever touched me before. But then, one day, I realized I liked it, and then you started hugging me, and I liked that too, but only after I felt like you weren't going to push me to pretend to love you."[1]

Brandi came to live with her parents at age thirteen and is now an adult: "Some of the hardest things to get used to were trying to meet their expectations of me. Nobody had ever held me accountable before and it was a new and unusual concept for me. It was also hard for me to have people in my business all the time. I wasn't used to involved parents, so that became very overwhelming. At first it made me feel untrusted, but then I came to cherish my parents' interest in my things. I also loved that they called me and introduced me as their daughter from day one. It took me almost two years before I called them Dad and Mom, but [to them] I was always their daughter."

When asked what adoptive parents can do to make the transition easier for their new children, she offered this advice: "Be patient. Most older-adopted kids are broken people. We don't trust easily and we are cautious. Once we feel secure and safe, we open up. Be kind. Harsh words and anger tend to hurt us more than the average person. For me, knowing I disappointed my parents was enough punishment. Be kind to yourself. You're going to make mistakes, but any parent will. Know that being a parent of an adopted child is harder and more emotional. Have faith in yourself and God. Know that all we as adoptees want is a loving, stable home."

Carissa Woodwyk (www.carissawoodwyk.wordpress.com) came home from Korea when she was four months old. Now, as an adult, she has many things that she wishes her parents and other adoptive parents understood about the heart of the adoptee. "I wish we would have talked more—about lots of things, but specifically about your adoption journey and my relinquishment journey. It would have been helpful to have had you wonder with me and ask questions with me and explore my heart with me and share your hearts with me. I minimized and dismissed so much inside of me, so much I was connected to, so much that was a part of me. Not your fault. Not my fault. It just happened. But it didn't have to happen.

"I know you didn't know. Maybe you didn't want to. Maybe it just felt distant and unimportant to you. Maybe you were trying to protect me, maybe yourselves, and keep us forward facing. But all the questions about my birth story and the two people who made me and the orphanage and foster home, all the shame that screamed in my head, all the rejection that veiled my footsteps into the world—it was there, deep inside. The people, the places, the noises, the smells—they were a part of me and a part of my story.

"And so, I had to find who I was, alone. I had to face my fear and shame, alone. I had to make sense of what happened, alone. I needed you beside me, drawing out my heart, pursuing my thoughts, giving me permission to feel and be curious and weep and ache. I needed hands to hold through the moments that I doubted my value, my life. I know you couldn't have rescued me or fixed it or made it better, but your presence, your voice of truth, your encouragement, your affirmation, your reminder of who I was and who I was created to be would have helped, would have sunk in.

"We could have experienced a richer, deeper, more intimate relationship if we could have gone there, to the hard places, together. Perhaps doing so would have changed all of us. So I grieve that this didn't happen. I don't blame you. I don't criticize you. I offer grace. I just wish it would have been different, because maybe I would have come to know Jesus' love for me sooner, trusted easier, loved more.

"Yet at the same time, in the honesty and disappointment of what didn't happen, I'm grateful beyond words for what you did offer me. You taught me how to step into life in strong and capable ways, moving forward with intent and wisdom, femininity and polish. The foundation you laid was safe and purposeful and moral and good in so many ways. You consistently pointed me upward. Thank you, from the bottom of my heart, for choosing the little baby with only a number for her name, bringing her home to your world, and loving her as best as you knew how. I got the best parts of you in me.

"Even though the beginning of my adoption story wasn't written with you, I have a strong belief that God is using that part of the story in beautiful and surprising ways. My story, our story—it's still being written. And it's a good story—one of truth and healing, redemption and love. One that shows and tells the world how good God is, how trustworthy His presence is, how available His love is . . . to everyone."

I remain confident of this:
I will see the goodness
of the LORD
in the land of the living.
PSALM 27:13

CHAPTER 10

Joy in the Journey

ONE DAY RECENTLY, AS I WAS SITTING IN THE BEDROOM working away at the tail end of this book, Lidya wandered in and flopped on the bed next to me to chat. Pretty soon Zeytuna came in, sat down on the bed, and joined the conversation. Ten minutes later, we were still chatting easily—no stress, no argument, just enjoying one another. And my heart just overflowed. For a time I honestly had to release the dream of having moments together like that. But here we are, our hearts growing together. The Lord has done great things for us, and we are filled with joy.

I've been encouraged along this path by other mothers who've shared stories of navigating challenges in their homes and helping their children grow along the way. Their issues may not be exactly like mine, but their successes and lightbulb moments have guided me on my own journey. So here in this last chapter, I wanted to share more of that type of encouragement—things that have worked well in our home and in the homes of others, and stories to encourage you on your way.

Have Fun Together

In the midst of helping a child settle in to the family, don't forget to fit in fun. One of the things I enjoy doing on a hard day is turning on some energetic or encouraging music and singing along. Sometimes I even grab a child by the hands and take a spin around the room with her. A cranky teen may roll his or her eyes at my goofiness, but often a smile perks around the edges anyway, and the mood is lightened.

What do you and your child truly enjoy doing together? Maybe it's playing Wii or painting your fingernails. Maybe it's running. Maybe it's shopping. Maybe you're both sci-fi buffs. The trick is to find things that you both honestly enjoy.

At our house games are often helpful. Phase Ten and Dutch Blitz are perennial favorites and can be played by large groups and a wide range of ages. Some of the craziest moments at our house involve a double pack of Dutch Blitz (highly recommended!) and a bunch of people laying down cards as fast as they can.

With teens it can be fun to find a TV show to watch together. John and I have found a couple of different shows that have reasonably good morals overall and a story line that engrosses everyone. Once a week or so, we'll stay up late and watch an episode or two together. Another thing I try to do now and then is invite a whole mob of teens over for a game night, a swim party, or a barbecue.

One interest that my teen daughters and I share is fashion.

Though clothes were a point of strife at first, these days both girls have a fabulous fashion sense and routinely come out of their bedroom in great outfits. We enjoy thrifting together. Sometimes I sneak in a bit of bonding time by asking their opinions about clothes in catalogs or on Pinterest. Often it gives me a bit more insight into their minds, and almost always it results in positive interaction.

I also like to ask the girls' advice about my own clothing. Even if the day has not gone well between us so far, they respond to the humility in my question, and will give me an answer that is both gentle and honest. I treasure those little times of sweet interaction because they remind me of all the growth that has happened since those hard early days. God is gracious.

> Martha Osborne, the founder of www.rainbowkids.com, said, "The challenge has been embracing that we are all the best we can be right now. I feel most successful as a mom when I positively communicate daily [with my kids]. One hug, one loving text, one something . . . something that says, 'I see you, I love you, you are amazing.' No matter what I get in return, what is going on in our lives, I feel I am investing in them, and the return for that investment sometimes comes back to me, and sometimes I just need to believe it will sink in and go forward for them."

Move It

Movement and fresh air help brains reset. A mini trampoline indoors, or a big one outdoors, is a great way to give kids a break when moods head south. Another way to get a fresh perspective is to send a child, or myself, or both of us off for a run. Sometimes I'll take a kid who's having a hard day along with me, and usually we end up being able to chat. Other times I choose to bring along a child who has been living in the background of the turmoil that day and needs some extra attention and focused momma time.

One day recently my youngest daughter was in a snit, and I wasn't sure why. I asked her to put on her shoes and come for a walk with me. At first she complained. But after we'd walked a bit, she started talking, first telling me what she was frustrated about, and then moving on to how she was going to raise her kids when she grew up. By the time we returned home, she was chattering away merrily, all traces of her previous unhappy mood completely gone. One-on-one time is precious, especially in a busy household.

Kate G. said, "I feel most successful and connected when I parent from the heart, rather than the head. When I can ignore the nagging voice in my head that says, 'Kids should behave in such and such a way' or 'It is absolutely unacceptable when kids do xyz'—and when I can really summon up feelings of love and caring. [For example] 'my son is acting a bit rudely and disrespectfully because he is hungry, and he always acts this way when he is hungry because it is a truly horrible feeling for him, and it's not because he is a bad kid.' When I can do that, the result is usually quite positive. I don't mean that I just let my son do whatever he wants or treat me however he wants to. But I've learned that whenever I get swayed by conventional notions of how 'good' kids behave, I am not as authentic with my own child. I stop listening to my instincts about what he truly needs from me. Someone might look at my son and think he is not exactly the most polite or well-behaved kid on the block. It's taken me a loooong time for that not to just drive me NUTS! But it's true—he isn't that 'perfect' kid. But he is MY kid, and after eight years together, it's good to realize that we are a success story for sure."

Lay Your Child's Future in the Arms of Jesus

A huge key to happiness as moms in the mucky middle of the parenting journey is continuing to appreciate our kids right where they are. I've met a lot of adoptive mommas. One thing we tend to have in common is that we are warriors on behalf of our children. Oh, we want good for them. It can hurt when we don't see progress. Haven't we proven ourselves trustworthy? Haven't we showered them with love? Why are they still using those wounded-child coping mechanisms?

Each repeat of difficult behavior can feel like more "evidence" that our child's future is going to be dysfunctional and full of pain and broken relationships. But the more we react in fear, the more our emotions get out of control, the more lies we believe, the harder it will be to love them joyfully just as they are.

Sure, we *want* our kids to be over their losses by now. But if they're not, they're not. Release the timing of that dream to God. Trust that whether you can see it or not, He is actively working in your child's life.

Do you long for your child to trust you as a parent? (Oh, how I wish for that very thing!) Then model trust by trusting in your heavenly Father. His plans will not be thwarted. He can mend your child's frail and torn heart. Be faithful day by day and trust the victory to Him.

Ashley (www.ashleykwells.com), momma to Jonathan and Jazmine in the previous chapter, said, "I have been so blessed by these children. They have shaped me in more ways than I can recount, and that has only been for the last eighteen months. I can't even imagine how much more they will change me as they continue to grow.

"I have been most surprised by the instant connection we had with our kids. It was visible even to outsiders looking in. At our first home visit with our case worker, she said that she has never seen or heard of children adjusting so quickly and so well to a new family. It truly was remarkable.

"What has been most challenging is coping with the demands of mothering four children, emotionally, mentally, physically. We were just thrown into parenthood, going from no children to four children within ninety minutes. Even still I am learning how to care for myself so that I do not get burnt out.

"My kids have taught me much about adoption and love in general. I thought I knew about love. It is a completely new ballgame to love in this way to children. I thought I understood God's love for me before. Now I understand it in a new way. When the kids do wrong against me, and I am tempted to become defensive or sensitive, I am having to put aside my own feelings for the well-being of the kids. I am having to choose to show love, even if at times I don't necessarily feel like showing love.

"Success at our house is a relative term. Lately, we are starting to see more moments of calm. We are having to remember to enjoy those moments, yet not expect them. We had about a week go by with no major problems, then we had many major blowouts in one day, and I was feeling so overwhelmed. In talking with my husband, I realized that I had allowed the previous week full of less chaos to become the new normal in my mind. Then I was thrown off course by a more realistic idea of family life. So, I am learning to savor the calm, yet expect the chaos."

Staying Softhearted

Most of us adoptive moms begin the journey with our hearts broken wide open with compassion. But after weeks or months or sometimes years of living with our wounded ones, something hard can happen even to well-intentioned hearts. The behavior birthed by their pain wounds us. The hurt steals peace from our home. It hurts others we love. Our compassion dwindles, and it feels like a battle against an enemy.

There is an enemy. But it isn't our children. There is a spiritual battle being waged for our children's souls. Satan wants to use the hurt in their pasts to make them bitter and scarred forever. We want them healed. Satan wants us to be so eaten up with hurt and resentment that we become unable to love our children well.

If your compassion begins to fade, remember who the enemy is. Pray for your child and over your child and with your child in the powerful name of Jesus. Remind yourself and your child that you are on the same side, fighting for love and relationship. Stay in the

Word every day. Read the Bible with your precious ones. Pray that God will give us His eyes and His love for them. He loves them (and us) perfectly, and has good plans for their futures.

> Beth Templeton, an adoptive mom who writes the blog hopeathome.org, said, "It never ceases to change my attitude to go over in my mind again the things God has said about my child. The promises, the scriptures, and the dreams that I know are in God's heart for this child. It takes my eyes off the circumstance of the now, which seem to be screaming against these very promises, and gives me vision again for what it is I am loving and sacrificing for— his freedom and healing and abundant life. It also helps me to remember that this is a process. The story is not over yet."

Remember to separate the child from his behavior. It's not as personal as we imagine. If your hurting child had been given to a different momma, his wounds would be pushing that mother away too. Sure, kids want to blame Mom for their troubles, but their greatest hurts happened before we ever entered their lives. And the God who never makes mistakes put us together for a reason. He believes I'm exactly the right parent for my child. Reminding myself of that truth lets me release the guilt I feel when I can't seem to "fix" hurting hearts.

I also try to remember moments when my children have expressed honest emotion with me and really shown me their souls. For some of us, those moments don't happen often. Hold them precious. One mom has a now-adult son who went through tremendous emotional pain in his teen years. She saved some of the voice mails he left on her phone during that time, because they take her back emotionally to a place where it was so easy for her to see his pain. Other moms remind themselves that the pain they're feeling is nothing compared to the pain their children felt at a very young and vulnerable ages.

> Lara said, "Our son has a pronounced flat spot on the back of his head from repeatedly slamming his head into the headboard of the tiny bed of the orphanage for stimulation up until he was four and we adopted him. He stopped doing that very shortly after we got him out; he started sleeping with us, and we were there to hold him. During toughest times with him, it finally occurred to me to consciously stroke his head so that I'd feel that spot and be reminded of what he suffered, putting myself into that time frame when I would have given anything to have been able to spare him that agony. It's like we have to co-suffer with them to help them heal."

Speaking Truth into Children's Hearts

Our children also need us to speak truth in their lives. Not long ago I was talking to my daughter, trying to figure out why she'd had a hard day; there'd been lots of disrespect and an attitude of unhappiness and discontent. I handed her the list of soul words mentioned earlier from the book *How We Love* and asked her to pick two words off the list that described how she was feeling. After ten minutes of looking at the page, she declared that her feelings weren't on the list. "That's okay," I said, "explain them to me."

Well, that was way too hard. She went back to looking at the list. Finally she managed to pick *annoyed* and *tired*: annoyed that people wanted to talk to her, and tired of talking to people. I said softly, "I'm sorry you're feeling annoyed, and I'm sorry that you're tired."

She looked at me with her eyebrows raised and said, "I doubt that."

There it was again: that lack of belief in my heart for her. I gently said, "It seems like you have a hard time believing I want good for you. I wonder why."

There was no answer.

I went on. "There's someone else you have a hard time believing good about. You know who?"

She looked mildly curious, but didn't offer a guess.

"It's you," I said. "Seems like it is really easy for you to believe bad about yourself too. But I want you to know you are a precious child of God. Not because of anything you did or didn't do, but because God made you and He loves you no matter what. And so do I. No matter what."

Our kids desperately need to hear that message of preciousness, even when, *especially* when, they are acting far from precious. Remember that awesome moment in the Bible when Jesus was coming up out of the water after being baptized, and the dove landed on Him? Remember what God said from the heavens? "This is My beloved Son, in whom I am well pleased" (Matt. 3:17 NKJV).

That's what we need to tell our kids over and over and over. Some days they won't listen and won't believe you; often a child who's struggling will reject your every attempt at encouragement. But whether they believe it or reject it, it's important to plant that seed of truth in their hearts anyway, and leave the growth to God.

Resting

For years when I was having a hard time with a child, I tried to reason him out of it. These days I'm slowly learning the value of silence. The other day when one of my children was struggling and refusing to talk to me about her frustration, I asked her to lie on the couch near me and just rest awhile. She flopped around for twenty minutes, still refusing to talk. Finally I turned on some praise music and spooned in behind her on the couch and just rested.

I'd been really frustrated, but the praise music let my heart be still. She isn't always open to touch, but lo and behold, she relaxed too. After twenty minutes or so she finally named a couple of feelings she had. We were able to move on with our day, and for the rest of the day there was an extra gentleness about her.

Oh, it is hard for me to just be still and wait. All my life I've handled difficulty by trying harder, doing more. But then God gave me kids whose hurts I couldn't "fix" no matter how hard I tried. Slowly He's teaching me that control is only a foolish illusion, one that leaves you miserable and frustrated, with gritted teeth and clenched fists.

It turns out that resting is actually where peace can be found. Wait. Fear not. Rest. He's got this covered. As it says in Isaiah 30:15, "In repentance and rest is your salvation, in quietness and trust is your strength."

If you feel helpless, hopeless, and broken, remember what is true. God is good, all the time. His promises never fail. He may or may not choose to completely heal our children. But He is with us every minute of the journey, and His plan is perfect.

A friend of mine struggling with the weariness in the parenting battle said that one day she realized Jesus was asking her, "Would you take this precious wounded one and love her, even if she never loves you back?"

Her answer was yes. So is mine.

In hard moments I find comfort in saying yes to that mission all over again. The desire of my heart is to joyfully serve my Savior with my life. This is what He has given me to do. And the really wonderful thing is that He's the one who gives me the grace to do it, to swing my feet out of bed every morning, stumble toward the coffee, and smile a greeting at kids who frown and kids who snuggle in for a hug and tell me about the crazy dream they had last night. To smile and hug and mother them all.

Some mornings exhaustion curtains my whole self. But I get up and set one foot in front of the other, doing love anyway. And partway through the morning, I'm sitting in a warm place with the sun at my back listening to a child reading me a story. And suddenly I realize my Savior has done it again. He's given me grace, new every morning. I lift my eyes to the Maker of the mountains I can't climb. And I thank Him.

Adoption and Siblings

At times I've been really sad about the strife that sometimes exists in our home due to parenting kids from hard places. I've experienced guilt that we didn't prepare our other children better, sadness that looking to the needs of grieving ones took time and attention away from our equally precious but quieter children. It has been a tough journey with many bumps and valleys, many winding rocky roads where I couldn't quite see our destination.

But God has "brought me out into a spacious place; he rescued me because he delighted in me" (Ps. 18:19). Over and over He shows me the good that has come to our kids as we've walked these hard paths, the lessons of sympathy and kindness and understanding that our children have been learning. These days one of the delights of my life is watching all our children interacting with one another.

Sure, there's arguing and unkindness sometimes among the younger ones still. But each and every child in the family has a sibling or two with whom they share a special bond, someone who makes them laugh or listens to their fears or teases them or hugs them around the neck when they get cranky. Through the very challenges that so much grieved my momma heart, God has been growing all our precious ones and creating a rich sense of loving community. What a gift.

Casey said, "I feel success most when we can really LAUGH together and enjoy each other. It really bonds you, doesn't it? That part was unexpected. Five years into our journey, it's those little 'family moments' that are also bonding us more and more . . . those memories that we can now share, laugh over, and shake our heads over. With my daughter who came home at five, I also feel success when she feels the freedom to be ornery with me, knowing then that she feels comfortable in her identity as a much-loved child. With my son who came home at nearly two years old but has exhibited more serious attachment-related issues, I feel success when I actually feel that spark of love that should be there naturally. Because we've gone through so much with him, I am so thankful when the Lord gives me those small feelings to keep me going."

Nurturing Momma

If you're not yet in the "wide place" where you can clearly see God's plan for your family, don't despair. If you catch yourself wondering if all this was a mistake, give yourself grace, and give your family time to adjust. Remember that bringing a new child into your family is a huge thing.

A few months ago you could probably sleep all night. You had more time to devote to your children, your spouse, yourself, your friends. Now, instead of spending your free time dreaming about a cherub who will run into your arms and be happy forever, you may be dealing with giardia and frequent night waking and tantrums and food issues. To top it all off, your kid may go rigid every time you hug him. No wonder you're grieving.

Grieving happens to every type of parent raising every type of child. But it is especially prevalent in parents whose kids are resisting bonding. Be aware that post-adoption depression is a real phenomenon. If you are struggling with your moods for weeks on end, talk to a trusted friend. Get a counselor. Arrange for respite on a regular basis, even if just for an afternoon a couple times a month. Some adoptive moms have found that short-term use of antidepressants was a blessing during a difficult adjustment period.

Probably the most important thing to do, though, is to rest in Jesus, keep praying, realize that your feelings are normal, and know you are not alone. Though some adoptive mommas can add children seemingly effortlessly, the majority of us experience growing pains as we help everyone in the family move toward a new normal.

The momma tends to be the hub of the home. We feel everyone's pain. We want so much for everyone to be happy, to feel loved and nurtured. But especially in the case of wounded children, we are not going to be able to fix everything. That can really leave us feeling drained. Because our job is so very pivotal, it is essential that we refuel regularly. We cannot nurture unless we ourselves are nurtured.

In those first months, or even years, after you have brought a child home, if you start to feel like you're falling to pieces, look to your self-care, and don't be afraid to tell your loved ones what kind of help you need. Are you staying in the Word? Cooking simply? Eating healthy food? Sleeping? Limiting kids' outside activities? Letting friends and relatives chauffeur kids essential places?

If you're up to your ears in young, needy children, you may need to hire a cleaning lady twice a month. Maybe you have a friend who would take five loads of laundry to the Laundromat for you once a week and bring it back folded. Maybe there's a neighborhood teen who'd be able to help some of your kids with homework in the afternoons.

Recharge, decompress, unwind, talk to trusted friends who've traveled this path and who won't judge you or your children. When I really need to vent, I speak with a dear friend who loves me and also adores my children, and has similar challenges in her own family. She can hear my complaints with sympathy, without judging me or my kids. She understands that I still greatly love my children, even as I am venting. We all need a safe friend like that. I am blessed to have her.

My mom is another safe listening ear. Sometimes we go for a brisk walk together and talk as we walk. I don't need to share every tiny bit of unhappiness I've experienced lately, but it's good to have an understanding ear to listen, occasionally give wise advice, and always point me toward Jesus. The better we can take care of ourselves, the better we'll be able to keep praying, keep loving, keep having hope even if growth seems slow.

Not long ago I was sitting in a coffee shop, working away on this last chapter of the book. My phone rang and I picked it up. It was Lidya, eighteen, calling me jubilant to tell me she'd gotten a 96 on an essay she'd written for her college psychology class. I was thrilled for her success. But I was even more thrilled that when this good thing had happened, one of her first thoughts had been to call me to share her happy moment. I am filled with joy to see this growth in our relationship.

On another day she gave me a suggestion to save a little bit of money on something. Then she laughed and said, "Wow, I sound like my mom!" My first thought was that she was talking about her first mom. But I realized she was referring to me. Her mom.

Wendy B. is the mother of nine children by adoption: "For my entire pre-married life, all I cared about was growing up and becoming a mom. When Tim and I were married, becoming a mother took on a whole new meaning for me. I was obsessed with it. With each miscarriage, I was heartbroken and distraught. There were days I felt I couldn't do one more moment of being a childless couple. And then God stepped in and blessed us with our first child, a baby girl born in Vietnam. My heart went from absolutely shattered to perfectly healed the moment she was placed in my arms. As I have been cleaning out the house, I have come across piles of photos of our beautiful children over the years. Each child is so precious to me. I can't help but tear up when I see the beautiful family that Tim and I, with God's help, have been able to create together. We are so very blessed. I have the family I always dreamed of. We may not look like each other, but we belong to one another and we are a family through and through. Sometimes we think we know what we want and need. But maybe that is not the plan God has for us. Maybe His plan is even better than we can imagine."

Back in 1997, when John and I began those first tentative adoption talks, I was imagining adopting one little girl. Little did we know that Lidya had already been born, and Josh, Ben, and Zeytuna would all be born the following year. Then later came our little ones. God's future for us was bigger than we ever could have imagined, but also more entwined with hurt than we ever could have seen.

We've grown and changed a lot since that first Christmas when I held that little fingerprint key chain in my hands. I realize ever more clearly that our true happily ever after won't come until heaven. There are lasting layers of pain that I didn't expect. But oh, the love is precious too.

These days those original four are grown. Amanda and Erika are both married, both with two little ones, which means John and I are now grandparents times four. Jared finishes college in 2014, and Daniel has a couple more years to go. They share an apartment with some friends and come to visit at least a couple Sundays a month.

We still have the youngest six at home. Josh, our first foray into adoption—the one whose easy transition emboldened our hearts for more adventure—still turns my heart to mush when he grins. Sometimes I can make him smile even when no one else can. He's learning to drive, is already taking some college classes, and wants to be a police officer someday.

Then there's Ben, my first experience with hard-won love. Trust was hard for him at first, but these days he never doubts I'm on his side. Our relationship is strong and good. He's been very easy to parent as a teen, something I would not have predicted back when he was a newly arrived toddler and we were struggling so hard. He has an easy wit, is a loyal friend, is a Harry Potter fanatic, and thinks he might train to work in prosthetics someday.

Emily, that serious toddler I worried so much about, is nearly twelve and softhearted as ever. She's almost as tall as I am and is good for a hug any minute of the day. She has a passion for arts and crafts, for her many friends, and for fashion design. Oh, she is a joy.

Our "baby" Julianna is almost into double digits and full of sass. Her siblings tell me I'm getting soft and she needs just a tad more discipline. They're probably right, but these "little" girls of ours are some of the easiest, most obvious gifts in my life. I love the way they come into my arms for a snuggle on the couch, bodies draped loose-limbed all over me. I love their sassy banter with their daddy, the easy affection that flows back and forth. We still have the teen years to navigate; there'll be hard moments and days. Even now there are hard moments, moments where she talks about missing her first family in Ethiopia. But the pure, easy momma love of my youngest two is a huge part of how God restores my soul on a daily basis. Our lives would have been so much poorer without them.

Then there is love even harder won, just beginning to bloom, promising much beauty. It's been a long journey since Lidya first sent me the little necklace symbolizing the hope of a daughter for a mother. She graduates from high school this year and is thinking about training to become a dental assistant. The other evening she was struggling with a tricky chemistry problem and was feeling frustrated. I patted the couch next to me and said, "Come sit and I'll help you."

She plopped down with the chemistry book, cranky, a couch cushion away. My forty-something eyes aren't that good, so I patted the spot right next to me again and said with a smile, "Come sit by me and pretend you like me."

I've made that joke before, and in the past it has fallen flat. But this time she laughed and plopped down shoulder to shoulder with me, still grinning. My heart sang. And then I helped her get un-stuck with her chemistry homework, and she continued to work companionably by my side even after she no longer needed my help.

That tiny moment right there—that's relationship. And she and I finally have it. God is so gracious to redeem my mistakes, to give us growth. He's put a new song in my heart, one full of gratitude deeper because this journey has been so much harder than I expected.

Our relationship, gnarled with snags and scars, places where the fit is not easy, is more precious to me because it is so hard-won. I understand more now about the depth of loss, about the way pain breaks hearts and makes loving again so hard. And yet here she is, brave enough to love me, her second momma. That's victory in Jesus, the God who redeems our lives from the pit. Oh, He has been good to us.

Zeytuna and I also are seeing amazing growth. I'm grateful for the writing of this book, to help me figure out some of my own stuck places, allowing me to be more openhanded, less reactive, more understanding, and (only by God's grace) more unconditional in my love. Already—or should I say finally?—I see signs of good things happening. She's talking to me these days, telling me when she's frustrated, even sometimes talking to me about judo or a con-versation with a friend. Going into deeper emotions is still hard for her, but I am so encouraged by the growth I'm seeing.

Awhile back I got going on a home improvement project that didn't go so well. I bent a lot of nails and dinged up a lot of wood in the process. When the project neared completion, I stood back and looked at it with my head cocked over to the side. Zeytuna came alongside me, head tipped sideways too. She squinted at my project and said, "It looks pretty good."

I told her I'd been doubting for a while that it'd be okay.

She looked me in the eye and said, "Yeah, lots of projects look kind of messy in the middle, but they usually work out okay in the end."

Do you know what it meant to me to have that child—out of all my ten—speak those words to me? I've struggled so hard to love her in a way that she can accept and felt so often like a failure at it. But at that moment it was as if God Himself was using my child's voice to whisper His truth in my ear, "It's going to be all right in the end."

As Christians we know it's going to be all right in the end, don't we? In fact, that's where we pin our faith: heaven is coming! And yet so often we judge our success as mothers by the muddled middle of our child's story. Or the muddled middle of our own story.

Never forget: our God is able to do immeasurably more than we can ever ask or hope or imagine according to His power that is at work within us.

Do not be weary in doing well, for in due time—after you get through the muddled middle—you *will* reap a reward if you do not faint. The King James Bible talks about fainting along the way, and I really appreciate that translation because so often as a momma I feel like today might be the day I faint along the way. Yet still He carries me.

Such hard times we've had. But each hard memory is an altar, an altar to God's faithfulness and the love that will not let us go. Remember all those altars they were always building in the Old Testament? They wanted to remember those places where God stepped in. You know what? So do I.

In all our lives, He's right there working. Let's remember that. He holds us, comforts us, redeems us, reminds us of His love, sends us forward with renewed faith and hope. He has redeemed our lives from the pit, and in the process He has given us a new song.

A Sunday or two ago everyone was at our house for lunch and an afternoon of visiting. Toddlers roamed the room making messes, trailed by teens tasked with supervising them. Babies were nursed by their mommas, then passed around among the aunts and uncles. Lidya sat tucked under an older brother's arm at the couch, chatting with him and playing with his cell phone. Josh and Ben were teasing and being teased by brothers-in-law. Zeytuna was in the periphery, quiet but drawn in to conversation now and then, sometimes reaching out to tease her favorite brother. Emily and Julianna were in bliss over having everybody home, visiting, playing with babies, chatting with everyone.

The dining table was blessedly, abundantly set for eighteen, with John and me all smiles to have everyone there. Maybe we won't all live close together always, but for now we are enjoying every minute of being together. Even the teens who sometimes despair of Mom and Dad feel that tangible sense of camaraderie on Sundays when the older siblings arrive. We are family. Jumbled and tumbled, pressed and tried, hearts full of memories both happy and sad, gathered together and grown together and sustained together by God on high. Family. We are incredibly blessed.

Let Me See Redemption Win

I think what we want most as parents is to know that there will be a happy ending, that all our sacrifices will pay off, that redemption will win. We dream of the day when our child seeks out our presence, lets us into her heart, smiles into our eyes, truly sees us as her forever mom. And as Christians we long for our children to embrace a saving faith in Jesus.

But whether we think we are seeing success or failure, we've got to remember this truth: Our hope is not in our child. Our hope is in the Lord. And with the Lord, redemption wins. He has promised to redeem all our pain, all our suffering, all our sadness and mistakes. He loves our children with an everlasting, perfect love. A love that can speak even to wounded hearts.

He's got it covered. Really.

And because He has it covered, redemption wins every time.

Whether or not we see a single glimmer of success before heaven, press on anyway. Our job is to show our kids His kind of love, to the best of our frail human ability. Yes, we're going to blow it. But wait a minute: here comes another try. Each minute we have a chance to vote "love," to reach out in love, to act in a way that builds connection, to set impatience aside, to ask forgiveness of our kids, and to try again.

We can go to bed every night confident that His grace covers it all, and wake up every morning trusting in that new-every-morning grace for this next day. Because we know there's an even greater redemption story than the one we're toiling over every day. It's the love story that led Jesus to the cross to die for us all. Even now He is doing a glorious work in all our lives. And someday we'll see the bigger picture.

Success might not look like we think it should. Not for years and years and years. But we know He's preparing a place for us in heaven, and we know His perfect love wins in the end. So go forward with faith. The God of angel armies is always by your side.

It's all Him. It's all Him.

Walk humbly. Love deeply. Be faithful. Don't lose hope.

He is mighty to save and He loves you and your precious children with an everlasting love. Don't be afraid of the muddle in the middle.

> *And it will be said in that day, "Behold, this is our*
> *God for whom we have waited that He might save*
> *us. This is the LORD for whom we have waited;*
> *Let us rejoice and be glad in His salvation."*
> ISAIAH 25:8 (NASB)

Notes

Chapter Two: Taking the Leap

1. IRS.gov, "Topic 607 - Adoption Credit and Adoption Assistance Programs," Updated December 12, 2013, www.irs.gov/taxtopics/tc607.html.
2. Insurance companies are required by law to insure adopted children just as they do birth children, pre-existing conditions and all.
3. User Mary Ostyn, Pinterest, Best Bunk Beds Ever board, Accessed April 8, 2014, www.pinterest.com/mary_ostyn/best-bunk-beds-ever.

Chapter Three: Building Heart Connections

1. *Empowered to Connect*, "A Journey of Faith—An Interview with Dr. Karen Purvis," Accessed April 8, 2014, www.empoweredtoconnect.org/a-journey-of-faith-an-interview-with-dr-karyn-purvis.
2. Ibid.
3. Robyn Gobbel, *Parenting. Adoption. Adoptive Parenting,* "You Must Jump Out of the Trauma Tornado," Posted March 18, 2013, www.gobbelcounseling.wordpress.com/2013/03/18/you-must-jump-out-of-the-trauma-tornado.
4. Dr. Karyn Purvis, David Cross, Wendy Sunshine, *The Connected Child* (Columbus, Ohio: McGraw-Hill Professional Publishing, 2007).

5. *A Parent's Guide to the Teen Brain*, "Adolescent Brain and Behavior," Accessed April 8, 2014, http://teenbrain.drugfree.org /science/behavior.html.

Chapter Five: Bringing Home Preschoolers and Older Children

1. David Albert, *Have Fun. Learn Stuff. Grow. Homeschooling and the Curriculum of Love* (Monroe, Maine: Common Courage Press, 2006).

Chapter Six: Sleeping and Eating and Date Nights, Oh My!

1. Susie Mesure, *The Independent*, "Penelope Leach: 'Face It: Babies Change Your Life,'" Posted May 6, 2010, www.independent.co .uk/life-style/health-and-families/features/penelope-leach -lsquoface-it-babies-change-your-lifersquo-1964429.html.
2. Elizabeth Pantley, *The No-Cry-Sleep Solution: Gentle Ways to Help Your Baby Sleep Through the Night* (New York: McGraw-Hill, 2002), 18.
3. Susan Emmett, Lillian Hudson, "And What About Food?" quoted in *Rainbowkids*, July 1, 2010, www.rainbowkids.com/ ArticleDetails.aspx?id=437.

Chapter Seven: When You're Down to Your Last Drop of Faith

1. Mary Sykes Wylie and Lynn Turner, *Psychotherapy Networker*, "The Attuned Therapist," Accessed April 7, 2014, www.psycho therapynetworker.org/magazine/recentissues/1261-the-attunded -therapist?start=5.
2. Daniel Siegel MD and Tina Payne Bryson PhD, *The Whole Brain Child* (New York, New York: Bantam Dell, 2012).
3. Dr. Laura Markham, *Aha! Parenting*, "For Parents: Healing Yourself," Accessed April 9, 2014, www.ahaparenting.com /parenting-tools/positive-discipline/healing-yourself.
4. Mary Sykes Wylie and Lynn Turner, "The Attuned Therapist," www.DrDanSiegel.com, Accessed April 9, 2014, http:// drdansiegel.com/uploads/The-attunded-therapist.pdf.

Chapter Eight: Beginning Again, at the Foot of the Cross

1. Carissa Woodwyk, *Restoration Living*, "A Story to Enter Into," Posted October 18, 2013, http://restorationliving.org/journal /a-story-to-enter-into.
2. Dr. Karyn Purvis, Together for Adoption Conference Breakout Session, Austin, Texas, November 2010.
3. Debra Delulio Jones, Christian Alliance for Orphans Summit, Breakout Session: Meltdown, May 2013, www.christianalliance fororphans.org/summit.
4. Some phrases adapted from Dr. Karyn Purvis, *Empowered to Connect Life Scripts*, www.empoweredtoconnect.org/wp-content /uploads/Life-Value-Scripts.pdf.

Chapter Nine: In Their Words: Thoughts from Adoptees

1. Cindy Lajoy, Lajoy Family Blog, "Angela's Adoption Advice," Posted March 13, 2013, www.lajoyfamily.blogspot.com/2013/04 /angelas-adoption-advice.html.

Acknowledgments

I WANT TO START BY THANKING MY FRIENDS IN THE adoption community whose comments added so much depth and interest to this book. Thank you, thank you for honestly sharing your joys and your challenges, and reminding us all that we're not alone. Thanks to my wonderful agent, Angela Miller, and the folks at Thomas Nelson Publishing for believing that this story needed to be told.

Thanks to my mom for showing me so much about being a good mom, for taking long walks with me on the hardest days, and for reminding me I don't have to be a perfect mom to be a good mom. Thanks to my dear husband, John, for being my biggest fan always, and during this project for reassuring me that it was okay to honestly talk about the hard bits right alongside the joyful.

Speaking of joy, I owe an incredible debt to the first moms of each of our adopted children for giving life to the precious children we share. I dream of a world where no mother would have to give up her child, and I will always remember your sacrifice. You are their forever moms too and hold a place of high honor in my heart and in their lives.

Thanks to my children for hanging in there with me as I learned more about loving you well, and for believing that my heart really is for you, even when I lose my cool. Oh, how I love each of you! I am so grateful for grace—the kind that we imperfect humans desperately need to extend to one another every day as we do life together—and the best grace of all, the kind offered by Jesus, who loves me even when I'm unlovable and who went to the cross to die. For me. And for you.

Amazing grace, how sweet the sound.

Appendix A:
Adoption Resources

OVER THE YEARS, WHILE LEARNING TO LOVE MY children well, I've been encouraged by many wise experts. Here are some of the books that I think every adoptive parent should read. If your reading time is limited, I'd encourage you to start at the top of the list and work your way down.

1. Karyn Purvis, David Cross, and Wendy Lyon Sunshine, *The Connected Child* (New York: McGraw-Hill, 2007).
2. Daniel Hughes, *Building the Bonds of Attachment* (Oxford: Rowan & Littlefield, 1998).
3. Daniel Siegel, *The Whole Brain Child* (New York: Bantam, 2012).
4. Daniel Siegel and Mary Hartzell, *Parenting From the Inside Out* (New York: Penguin, 2003).
5. Deborah Gray, *Attaching in Adoption* (London: Jessica Kingley Publishers, 2012).

6. Karyn Purvis, *Trust-Based Parenting* (DVD series).

7. Carol Lozier, LCSW, *The Adoptive and Foster Parent Guide* (Createspace, 2012).

8. Milan and Kay Yerkovich, *How We Love Our Children* (Colorado Springs: WaterBrook Press, 2011).

9. Jayne Schooler, *Wounded Children, Healing Homes* (Colorado Springs: NavPress, 2010).

10. Robert Karen, *Becoming Attached* (New York: Oxford University Press, 1998).

Appendix B:
Playlist for a Weary Momma

MUSIC HAS POWER TO SOOTHE THE SOUL. HERE ARE SOME
of the songs that have spoken God's truth and hope into my heart
in hard moments during recent years. For an update on my list, visit
the songs page on my blog: http://owlhaven.net/music.

Meredith Andrews, "Not for a Moment"
Tenth Avenue North, "Worn"
Laura Story, "Make Something Beautiful"
Kari Jobe, "Steady My Heart"
Group 1 Crew, "His Kind of Love"
Sovereign Grace Music, "Glorified"
Bebo Norman, "I Will Lift My Eyes"
Pocket Full of Rocks, "At the Cross"
Jeremy Camp, "Reckless"
Laura Story, "God of Every Story"
Tenth Avenue North, "Strangers Here"
Sara Groves, "When It Was Over"

Grey Holiday, "You Belong To Me"
Laura Story, "What a Saviour"
Mark Gungor, "Beautiful Things"
Newsboys, "Build Us Back"
Natalie Grant, "Your Great Name"
Laura Story, "He Will Not Let Go"
Matthew West, "Waiting on a Miracle"

Appendix C:
More Ways to Love Orphans

DURING MY YEARS IN THE ADOPTION COMMUNITY, I'VE been blessed to encounter amazing people and organizations that are passionate about supporting orphans and widows. We may not all be called to adopt, but we are all called to help the widow and the orphan in their distress (James 1:27). Here are a few of my very favorite agencies committed to orphan care, family preservation, and improving life in poverty-ridden communities. If you are looking for ways to love orphans in the name of Jesus, please consider supporting these fine organizations.

Compassion International: http://compassion.com
Compassion International is a child sponsorship program that supports children so that they can remain in school and provides them a meal a day, which decreases the burden on their families.
In 2008, I had the privilege of visiting several Compassion projects in the Dominican Republic and was amazed by all they do for the children there.

Bring Love In: http://bringlove.in

    Bring Love In was founded by Levi and Jessie
    Benkert to serve widows and orphans in Ethiopia.
    They are bringing widows together with orphans and
    creating new families and also are providing financial
    support to families who are living on the edge so that
    they do not have to relinquish their children to be
    raised by others.

The Charis Project: http://thecharisproject.org

    Carrien and Aaron Blue began the Charis Project to
    support a series of children's homes in Thailand with
    the goal of eventually making each children's home
    self-sufficient. They do this by providing job training,
    business advice, and start-up funding for cottage
    businesses for the operators of each children's home.

Equip missionary, Sophie Ness: http://www.equip
  international.com

    Sophie is my youngest sister. She is doing medical
    mission work in a rural community in southern
    Ethiopia. She works primarily with pregnant women,
    providing prenatal care and malaria treatment with
    the goal of decreasing the maternal mortality rate.
    She also does postpartum checks and provides
    extra nutrition to mothers of twins so that they can
    successfully nurse their babies. She is hoping to
    gradually increase the number of women in her care.
    Sophie blogs at sophinafrica.com.

About the Author

MARY OSTYN IS A DYNAMIC YET DOWN-TO-EARTH author and speaker who is passionate about encouraging women in all stages of their mothering journeys. After a decade as a registered nurse in labor and delivery, she now encourages mommas via books, speaking, and her blog at www.owlhaven.net. She lives with her high school sweetheart in Nampa, Idaho, where she homeschools the youngest six of their ten children, including four daughters born in Ethiopia and two sons born in South Korea.